THE VIETNAM WAR FOR TEENS

Amazing Facts, Heroic Acts, Major Events, Public Protest, and How the War Changed America

James Burrows

© **Copyright 2025 - All rights reserved.**

The content contained within this book may not be reproduced, duplicated or transmitted without direct written permission from the author or the publisher.

Under no circumstances will any blame or legal responsibility be held against the publisher, or author, for any damages, reparation, or monetary loss due to the information contained within this book, either directly or indirectly.

Legal Notice:

This book is copyright protected. It is only for personal use. You cannot amend, distribute, sell, use, quote or paraphrase any part, or the content within this book, without the consent of the author or publisher.

Disclaimer Notice:

Please note the information contained within this document is for educational and entertainment purposes only. All effort has been executed to present accurate, up to date, reliable, complete information. No warranties of any kind are declared or implied. Readers acknowledge that the author is not engaged in the rendering of legal, financial, medical or professional advice. The content within this book has been derived from various sources. Please consult a licensed professional before attempting any techniques outlined in this book.

By reading this document, the reader agrees that under no circumstances is the author responsible for any losses, direct or indirect, that are incurred as a result of the use of the information contained within this document, including, but not limited to, errors, omissions, or inaccuracies.

Other Books by James Burrows

What You Need To Know:

World War I for Teens
World War I for Kids
World War II for Teens
World War II for Kids
World War II for Teens – 21 Special Operations
World War II for Teens – The Secret War
World War II for Teens – The Holocaust
World War II – The Pacific War
The Vietnam War for Teens

The Ultimate Guide:

Egyptian Mythology for Kids
Greek Mythology for Kids
Norse Mythology for Kids

Concise Guides:

A History of Israel and Palestine
Alexander the Great - One Man. One Empire. One Legacy.

Other Books:

The Art of War – Sun Tzu
Meditations – Marcus Aurelius

CONTENTS

INTRODUCTION

1. VIETNAM'S COLONIAL PAST AND THE ROAD TO CONFLICT

I. Setting the Scene
II. French Colonization of Vietnam
III. The Rise of Vietnamese Nationalism
IV. World War II and the End of French Rule in Vietnam
V. The Geneva Accords and the Division of Vietnam

2. THE COLD WAR AND U.S. INVOLVEMENT

I. The Struggle Between Communism and Capitalism
II. The Domino Theory: The Fear of Communism Spreading Across Southeast Asia
III. Early U.S. Support: Advisors and Limited Involvement in the 1950s
IV. The Gulf of Tonkin Incident: The Catalyst for Full-Scale Escalation

3. A WAR OF IDEOLOGIES - WHO WAS INVOLVED

I. The Viet Cong and North Vietnamese Army
II. The U.S. and the Army of the Republic of Vietnam (ARVN)
III. The Soviet Union and China
IV. The United States

4. KEY EVENTS AND TIMELINE OF THE WAR

I. 1954-1960: The Seeds of Conflict
II. 1961-1964: Escalation of U.S. Involvement
III. 1965-1968: Escalation and Turning Points
IV. 1969: Nixon Takes Office and Begins Vietnamization
V. 1970: Invasion of Cambodia and the Expansion of the War
VI. 1971: Pentagon Papers Leak and Growing Domestic Opposition
VII. 1972: The Easter Offensive and Vietnamization's Limits
VIII. 1972: The Christmas Bombing and Operation Linebacker

IX. 1973: The Paris Peace Accords and U.S. Withdrawal
X. 1975: The Fall of Saigon and the End of the War

5. THE WAR IN NUMBERS

I. American Forces in Vietnam
II. South Vietnam's Army: The ARVN
III. North Vietnamese and Viet Cong Forces
IV. Civilian and Military Casualties
V. American Casualty Statistics and the Human Dimension
VI. Prisoners of War (POWs): Stories of Resilience and Survival
VII. Honors: Recognizing Bravery and Sacrifice
VIII. Technology: Helicopters, Napalm, and Unexploded Ordnance
IX. Financial Cost: An Expensive Conflict
X. Protests: The Anti-War Movement and the Moratorium March
XI. The Technicality of "War" Status

6. LIFE AS A SOLDIER

I. Draft and Recruitment: The Mobilization of Young Soldiers
II. The Jungle Environment, Combat, Tunnel Rats, and Morale
III. War Heroes

7. THE WAR BACK HOME

I. The Growing Anti-War Movement: Origins and Protests
II. Who Was Involved in the Anti-War Movement
III. Media Coverage: Bringing the War Into American Living Rooms

8. THE SOCIAL CHANGES IN AMERICA

I. Civil Rights and the Vietnam War
II. Youth and the Counterculture Movement
III. Impact on Veterans

9. THE END OF THE WAR AND ITS AFTERMATH

I. The U.S. Withdrawal and the Fall of Saigon: The Costs and Consequences of the

Vietnam War
II. The Costs of War
III. Vietnam After the War: Rebuilding and the Path to Economic Reform

10. THE LEGACY OF THE VIETNAM WAR

I. Vietnam Syndrome and Changes in U.S. Foreign Policy
II. Vietnam in Popular Culture
III. How the Vietnam War Shaped Modern America
IV. Remembering Vietnam: Memorials, Recognition, and Enduring Lessons

11. EPILOGUE: REFLECTIONS AND LESSONS OF THE VIETNAM WAR

I. Key Takeaways: Political and Social Lessons
II. Quotes from Veterans and Protesters: Reflections from Those Affected
III. Remembering and Learning from the Vietnam War

ABOUT THE AUTHOR

INTRODUCTION

Hey there! If you're holding this book, chances are you're curious about the Vietnam War. Maybe you've heard about it in school, seen a movie, or had someone in your family mention it. But what is it, really? Why do people still talk about a war that ended decades ago?

Here's the thing: the Vietnam War wasn't just a series of battles fought halfway across the world. It was one of the most complex and consequential events in modern history, shaping not only the fate of Vietnam but also profoundly impacting the social, political, and cultural fabric of the United States and other nations. It is a conflict deeply rooted in a long history of struggle, resilience, and change, and its legacy continues to echo through the world today.

And let's be real: wars can sound like a lot of dates and facts on paper. But behind every event are real people - young people like you - facing choices, challenges, and changes that shaped their lives forever.

In this book, we're going to take a journey through the Vietnam War: why it started, what it was really like for the soldiers fighting, and how it left a mark on the world. We'll explore the action on the battlefield, but also what was happening in homes, classrooms, and in society back in the U.S.

So, grab a seat, and let's dive into a story about courage, mistakes, heartbreak, and hope. Because the Vietnam War isn't just history - it's a story that still matters today.

The Relevance of the Vietnam War Today

The Vietnam War - sometimes called the Second Indochina War - didn't just appear out of nowhere in the 1950s when the U.S. first got involved. Its roots go much deeper, tied to Vietnam's fight for independence and the bigger global showdown known as the Cold War.

After World War II, the world was basically split into two camps: the capitalist United States and the communist Soviet Union. These two superpowers were in a constant tug-of-war, trying to spread their influence and outmaneuver each other. Unfortunately for Vietnam, its struggle for freedom from colonial rule ended up right in the middle of this global rivalry.

What started as a fight for independence turned into a long, bloody conflict, with Vietnam caught between local struggles and superpower politics. It was a clash of big ideas - freedom, communism, democracy - but also about ordinary people trying to shape their own future.

Ideas vs Ideologies

Understanding the Vietnam War is crucial today because it was not just a battle over territory or resources; it was a struggle over ideas and ideologies, such as democracy versus communism, individual rights versus collective welfare, and the limits of government power. These are issues that continue to shape politics and society today.

In many ways, the Vietnam War serves as a case study in the complexities and unintended consequences of foreign intervention. The U.S. government entered the conflict with the belief that it was protecting democracy and containing communism, but the war quickly became a quagmire, leading to deep divisions within the United States and sparking one of the most significant anti-war movements in history. The Vietnam War today still offers lessons on the importance of questioning government actions, especially when they involve issues of war and peace.

Private Michael J Mendoza Firing His M16, Vietnam

Impact on American Society

One of the most important legacies is the impact on American society. For the first time, television brought the realities of war into people's homes, and many Americans were horrified by the images of death and destruction they saw. The war caused a generational divide, with younger Americans often more skeptical of the government's motives and more willing to protest.

The anti-war movement in the United States became a powerful force, with students, civil rights leaders, and even veterans joining together to call for an end to the war. This movement helped to change the way Americans view their government and their role in the world, leading to a more questioning and less trusting society.

The Psychological Toll of Warfare

Soldiers paid a heavy psychological toll. Many returned home with physical injuries, but an equally large number suffered from mental health issues, including what is now known as post-traumatic stress disorder (PTSD). This recognition of the "invisible wounds" of war has had lasting effects on how we think about mental health, particularly for veterans.

Reconciliation and Healing

The war's aftermath offers important lessons in reconciliation and healing. After the U.S. withdrew from Vietnam, the country faced years of rebuilding and reconciliation. The communist government implemented policies to unite the country and rebuild its economy, but this process was slow and challenging.

In the decades since the war, Vietnam has moved toward a more open, market-oriented economy, improving the lives of millions of people. The relationship between the United States and Vietnam has also transformed from one of animosity to one of cooperation.

Cultural Understanding and Diplomacy

For young people today, the Vietnam War offers a powerful lesson about the importance of cultural understanding and diplomacy. A big part of what fueled the conflict was a failure to truly understand Vietnamese culture and history. Many U.S. leaders at the time saw the war purely as a fight against communism, overlooking the deep desire of the Vietnamese people for independence and self-determination. This lack of cultural awareness led to serious mistakes and misunderstandings, which ended up prolonging the war and making it far more devastating for everyone involved.

In an increasingly globalized world, learning from these mistakes is essential. It reminds us that understanding and respecting other cultures is crucial in avoiding conflict and building lasting peace.

The Human Cost of War

Finally, the Vietnam War serves as a reminder of the human cost of war. The conflict resulted in the deaths of millions of Vietnamese people, as well as tens of thousands of U.S. soldiers. It left lasting scars on the land, with unexploded bombs and toxic chemicals like Agent Orange continuing to harm people in Vietnam decades later. It underscores the importance of seeking peaceful solutions to conflicts and the need for compassion and empathy in international relations.

The Vietnam War is a powerful chapter in history that had a lasting impact on both Vietnam and the United States. It's not just about dates or battles - it's about the deeper themes of courage, resilience, and the fight for justice that still resonate today. For Vietnam, it's the story of a small nation standing its ground against overwhelming odds, determined to claim its independence and self-determination. For Americans, it's a sobering reminder of why it's so important to question authority, seek the truth, and truly understand the heavy price of war.

After reading this book, you will know:

- The causes of the war and who was involved.
- The Domino Theory and the fear of communism.
- How the 'Draft' worked in America and why it was controversial
- How Agent Orange and Napalm were used by the U.S.
- How the anti-war movement developed across America
- The human, economic and political costs of the war

❖*DID YOU KNOW*

Look out for incredible war facts throughout the book, some amazing, some weird, some horrible and some just mind-boggling!

Let's drop into the jungle and find out everything we can about the war that changed America!

1. VIETNAM'S COLONIAL PAST AND THE ROAD TO CONFLICT

I. Setting the Scene

Map of Vietnam

Firstly, let's get some background on Vietnam. Situated in Southeast Asia, Vietnam is bordered by China to the north, Laos and Cambodia to the west, and the South China Sea to the east. This region, often referred to as Indochina, has been a crossroads of cultures and influences for centuries. Its location made Vietnam a key player in regional trade routes, and its lush landscapes and fertile lands were attractive to neighboring powers and, later, to European colonizers.

Terraced fields, Vietnam

Vietnam's topography varies widely, from the low, sprawling rice fields in the south's Mekong Delta to the rugged highlands in the north, creating a land rich in natural beauty and resources. The culture of Vietnam is equally rich, shaped by centuries of interaction with neighboring China, Southeast Asian nations, and later, France.

Hanoi today

Vietnamese culture is known for its deep traditions, with Confucian and Buddhist values at its heart, emphasizing family, respect for elders, and a harmonious relationship with nature. These values can be seen in daily life, from the way Vietnamese families operate to the beautiful pagodas and temples scattered across the country. Vietnamese art, literature, and food are a unique blend of indigenous elements and outside influences, creating a vibrant cultural identity that is deeply cherished by its people.

However, Vietnam's history has been marked by almost constant conflict and struggle for independence. For more than a thousand years, Vietnam was under the domination of China, during which time Chinese culture and government systems heavily influenced the region. This influence is still visible today in aspects of Vietnamese language, cuisine, and traditions. Despite this long period of control, the Vietnamese people maintained a fierce desire for independence, resisting Chinese rule through multiple rebellions and developing a national identity rooted in resilience and self-reliance.

In the 19th century, Vietnam faced a new wave of foreign dominance, this time from European colonizers. The French took control of Vietnam in the mid-1800s as part of their larger empire in Indochina, seeking to exploit the country's natural resources and establish a foothold in Southeast Asia. Resistance to French rule grew steadily, with nationalist leaders like Ho Chi Minh eventually emerging to champion the cause of Vietnamese independence.

◻ *DID YOU KNOW*

- Vietnam has a population of 99 million

- At its narrowest, Vietnam is only 30 miles wide while its coastline in the east, stretches to 1,000 miles!

- Over 2,360 rivers flow through Vietnam, including the iconic Mekong River and the Red River.

- Vietnam is the world's 2nd largest exporter of coffee and the largest exporter of cashew nuts and black pepper.

II.◻*French Colonization of Vietnam*

The Beginning of French Control in Vietnam

French colonization in Vietnam began in the 1850s, a period marked by increasing European influence across Southeast Asia. France sought to expand its empire, motivated by the desire to exploit new markets, establish a stronger presence in Asia, and promote its cultural and political ideals. Vietnam, with its strategic location and resources, became a target of French ambition.

The colonization process officially started with France's military intervention in 1858, justified by the French as a protective move to defend the Christian missionaries in Vietnam, who were allegedly persecuted by the ruling Nguyen Dynasty. However, beneath this veneer of religious protection, the French sought economic and political control.

The Nguyen Dynasty, which ruled Vietnam at the time, struggled to resist French military superiority. After several battles and escalating tensions, Vietnam formally became a French colony in 1887 with the creation of French Indochina, which included present-day Vietnam, Laos, and Cambodia. This transformation drastically altered Vietnam's political, economic, and social landscape, as French colonial rule imposed foreign governance structures and economic practices that prioritized French interests.

Reshaping Vietnamese Society and Politics

Under French rule, Vietnamese society and politics were dramatically changed. The French colonial administration divided Vietnam into three distinct regions: Tonkin in the north, Annam in the center, and Cochinchina in the south. Each region was governed differently, with Cochinchina becoming a directly administered colony, while Annam and Tonkin operated as protectorates, allowing the Vietnamese emperor to retain nominal power but under strict French supervision. This division hindered the unity of Vietnam and facilitated French control, as local identities and regional disparities were manipulated to maintain colonial dominance.

Economically, the French introduced large-scale agricultural and industrial projects, focusing on rubber, rice, and other cash crops. These industries primarily served French economic interests and were sustained by the labor of Vietnamese peasants, who faced exploitation, land dispossession, and harsh working conditions. The French colonial administration enforced a land tax system that placed significant financial burdens on the Vietnamese population, often leading to the concentration of land ownership in the hands of a few wealthy landlords and exacerbating poverty among rural communities. This economic disparity fueled discontent and sowed the seeds of resistance.

Socially and culturally, French colonization attempted to impose European values and educational systems. The French established schools in Vietnam to promote French language and culture, aiming to create a Westernized elite who could serve as intermediaries between the colonial rulers and the Vietnamese populace. While some Vietnamese embraced French education and even admired aspects of French culture, others viewed this as an erosion of Vietnamese identity. The French also implemented policies that gave privileges to French citizens and a small group of Westernized Vietnamese elites, marginalizing the majority of the population and creating deep divisions within society.

Political Suppression and Resistance

Politically, the French colonial administration imposed strict controls to suppress any form of dissent. Nationalist movements and attempts to promote Vietnamese sovereignty were met with harsh repression, censorship, and imprisonment. The French established a network of police and intelligence agencies to monitor potential threats, and political opponents were often arrested or exiled. However, these repressive measures did not completely quell the growing sentiment for independence, which began to take root among various segments of Vietnamese society.

As time went on, the Vietnamese populace grew increasingly disillusioned with French colonial rule. The hardships of colonial exploitation, coupled with the desire to preserve Vietnamese cultural identity, ignited a sense of nationalism. Although the French tried to maintain control through a mixture of force and cultural assimilation, they inadvertently fostered a new generation of Vietnamese thinkers, intellectuals, and activists who would become instrumental in the country's fight for independence.

III. The Rise of Vietnamese Nationalism

The Early Nationalist Movement

The desire for Vietnamese independence was rooted in the long-standing resistance to foreign dominance. Vietnamese history is marked by resistance against invaders, particularly against the Chinese, who had ruled Vietnam for over a thousand years before Vietnamese leaders reclaimed their independence. This legacy of resistance played a crucial role in shaping Vietnamese identity, creating a foundation for the nationalist movement against French colonial rule.

The nationalist movement initially took the form of secret societies and regional uprisings. Early nationalist leaders, including Phan Boi Chau and Phan Chu Trinh, advocated for reform and resistance in various ways. Phan Boi Chau, influenced by anti-colonial movements worldwide, called for violent resistance to overthrow French rule. In contrast, Phan Chu Trinh believed in a gradual approach to modernization, advocating for educational and social reforms to empower the Vietnamese people within the colonial system. Both approaches gained followers, and their efforts laid the groundwork for future resistance movements.

Ho Chi Minh and the Formation of Revolutionary Ideals

Ho Chi Minh

The most prominent figure in the Vietnamese independence movement was Ho Chi Minh, born Nguyen Sinh Cung in 1890. Ho Chi Minh's journey to becoming the leader of Vietnamese nationalism was shaped by his experiences abroad. As a young man, he traveled to France, where he was exposed to socialist and anti-colonial ideas. Witnessing the inequalities within the French empire, Ho Chi Minh became deeply committed to the cause of Vietnamese independence and the broader fight against imperialism.

In 1920, Ho Chi Minh joined the French Communist Party, seeing communism as a way to unite the working class against colonial oppressors. He believed that Marxist ideology could offer a path toward Vietnamese independence by mobilizing the peasants and workers who had suffered under colonial exploitation. Throughout the 1920s and 1930s, he organized and mobilized Vietnamese expatriates in France, the Soviet Union, and China, spreading revolutionary ideas and fostering connections with other anti-colonial movements.

◻ *DID YOU KNOW*

- For 3 years, from 1911, Ho Chi Minh worked on a French steamer as a cook, visiting various African ports, and Boston and New York.

- 1917, he moved to France, working as a gardener, sweeper, waiter, photo retoucher and oven stoker.

- In 1919, he sent a petition to the great powers at the Versailles Peace Conference after WW1, demanding equal rights for the Vietnamese from its French rulers.

In 1941, Ho Chi Minh returned to Vietnam and founded the Viet Minh (Vietnam Independence League), a coalition of nationalist and communist forces committed to ending French rule. As we will see in the next section, during World War II, the Japanese occupation of Vietnam weakened French control, creating an opportunity for the Viet Minh to gain power. The Viet Minh capitalized on this moment, rallying support among the Vietnamese population by emphasizing the ideals of independence, social equality, and resistance against foreign occupation.

IV.◻World War II and the End of French Rule in Vietnam

The Impact of World War II on Colonial Powers

World War II fundamentally weakened European colonial powers, reshaping the global landscape and giving rise to strong anti-colonial movements in Asia, Africa, and beyond. For France, the war and subsequent occupation by Nazi Germany left the country economically devastated and politically fractured. This vulnerability was especially apparent in French colonies, where resistance movements began to gain momentum as colonial governments weakened. Vietnam, part of French Indochina, became a focal point of resistance and change during this period, setting the stage for France's eventual departure.

In 1940, following the German occupation of France, Japan took advantage of the situation by pressuring the Vichy government in France to allow Japanese troops to station in Vietnam. France, unable to defend its colonial territories, reluctantly agreed, and Vietnam came under joint French and Japanese control. Although the French administration remained in place, it functioned largely under Japanese authority, losing substantial control over local affairs. For the Vietnamese, this dual occupation created an atmosphere of confusion and exploitation, deepening local resentment toward colonial rule.

As Japan's grip on Vietnam tightened, the Japanese exploited the country's resources to fuel their war efforts. Vietnam's agricultural output, particularly its rice production, was redirected toward Japan, creating severe shortages for local populations. The situation reached a critical point in 1945 when a massive famine, exacerbated by Japanese exploitation and natural disasters, resulted in the deaths of an estimated two million Vietnamese. This humanitarian crisis intensified Vietnamese anger toward foreign occupiers and galvanized anti-colonial sentiment, leading many to seek independence from both Japanese and French rule.

The Rise of the Viet Minh and Ho Chi Minh

In response to this period of hardship and turmoil, the Viet Minh emerged as a powerful force, bringing together various factions, including communists, nationalists, and other anti-colonial groups, united in their desire to end foreign rule in Vietnam. Ho Chi Minh, an influential figure with experience in international revolutionary circles, saw the Japanese occupation as an opportunity to build momentum for Vietnam's liberation.

Throughout World War II, the Viet Minh waged a guerrilla campaign against both the Japanese occupiers and the weakened French administration. They established strongholds in rural areas, gaining support among the peasantry, who saw the Viet Minh as champions of Vietnamese independence and justice. As World War II neared its end, the Viet Minh's influence grew, positioning them as a legitimate opposition to foreign rule.

In August 1945, after the Japanese surrender following the bombings of Hiroshima and Nagasaki, the Viet Minh seized their moment. With the power vacuum left by the retreating Japanese forces, the Viet Minh launched the August Revolution, mobilizing forces to capture key cities and towns across Vietnam. On September 2nd, 1945, Ho Chi Minh declared Vietnamese independence in Hanoi, delivering a speech that referenced both the American Declaration of Independence and the French Declaration of the Rights of Man and of the Citizen. It marked the establishment of the Democratic Republic of Vietnam (DRV), which Ho Chi Minh hoped would be recognized by the international community.

France's Attempt to Reclaim Control

While the declaration of independence was a pivotal moment, it did not mean the immediate end of French control in Vietnam. After Japan's surrender, the Allied powers, primarily Britain and China, agreed that France would resume control of its colonies in Southeast Asia. In 1946, French forces returned to Vietnam, determined to reassert their authority. This move was met with resistance from the Viet Minh, who viewed the reestablishment of French rule as a betrayal of their struggle for independence.

The situation quickly escalated into open conflict, marking the beginning of the First Indochina War (1946-1954). This conflict, driven by the Viet Minh's desire for independence and France's determination to retain its colonial empire, was brutal and protracted. French forces held control over major cities, while the Viet Minh operated in rural areas, using guerrilla tactics to wear down French forces. The war placed a significant strain on both France and Vietnam, and its outcome would have far-reaching consequences for the future of the region.

The First Indochina War and France's Defeat at Dien Bien Phu

The First Indochina War raged on for eight years, with neither side able to gain a decisive advantage. The French forces, although technologically superior, struggled to combat the Viet Minh's guerrilla tactics, which relied on surprise attacks, mobility, and popular support among the Vietnamese population. Ho Chi Minh and General Vo Nguyen Giap, a brilliant military strategist, led the Viet Minh forces, adapting strategies that maximized their advantages and minimized their weaknesses against the French.

The turning point of the war came in 1954 at the Battle of Dien Bien Phu, where French forces suffered a devastating defeat. This remote area in northern Vietnam, was chosen by the French as a strategic stronghold to cut off Viet Minh supply lines and crush their forces. However, the French underestimated the Viet Minh's determination and logistical capabilities. General Giap organized a massive siege, transporting heavy artillery over rough terrain to encircle the French position. The battle lasted nearly two months and ended with a French surrender on May 7th, 1954. This defeat shocked France and made it clear that their colonial ambitions in Vietnam were no longer tenable.

◻ *DID YOU KNOW*

- French forces suffered 74,200 deaths in the First Indochina war.

- It's estimated that between 175,000 and 300,000 Vietnamese were killed or went missing.

The loss at Dien Bien Phu was a decisive factor in forcing France to negotiate with the Viet Minh. The end of the First Indochina War marked the end of French colonial rule in Vietnam and signaled a shift in global attitudes toward colonialism. France's defeat demonstrated that colonial powers could be overthrown by determined nationalist movements, inspiring similar movements across Asia and Africa.

V.◻ *The Geneva Accords and the Division of Vietnam*

The Geneva Conference

In the aftermath of the First Indochina War, representatives from several countries gathered in Geneva, Switzerland, in 1954 to negotiate a settlement for Indochina.

This conference, known as the Geneva Conference, included representatives from France, the Democratic Republic of Vietnam (DRV), the United States, the Soviet Union, China, and other nations. The purpose of the conference was to establish a framework for peace in Vietnam and to address the broader issue of decolonization in Southeast Asia.

The conference lasted from April to July 1954, with delegates working to find a solution that would satisfy both the French and the Viet Minh, as well as the interests of major global powers. One of the central issues was how to handle the political and ideological divisions in Vietnam. While the Viet Minh sought a unified, independent Vietnam under their control, Western powers feared the spread of communism and wanted to prevent Ho Chi Minh's influence from extending throughout the country.

The Division of Vietnam at the 17th Parallel

The Geneva Accords, signed on July 21st, 1954, formally ended the First Indochina War and outlined the terms for peace. The most significant outcome of the Accords was the temporary division of Vietnam into two separate zones along the 17th parallel, roughly halfway between the north and south of the country.

According to the agreement:

- The North: The Democratic Republic of Vietnam, led by Ho Chi Minh and the Viet Minh, would govern the northern half of the country, with its capital in Hanoi.

- The South: The southern half of Vietnam would be governed by the State of Vietnam, an anti-communist regime led by Emperor Bao Dai and supported by Western allies, particularly the United States. The southern capital was established in Saigon.

This division was intended to be temporary, with the Geneva Accords calling for national elections to be held in 1956 to reunify the country under a single government chosen by the Vietnamese people. However, deep political and ideological divisions between the North and South made this goal difficult to achieve. While the Viet Minh anticipated that elections would solidify their control over a unified Vietnam, the anti-communist government in the South, backed by the United States, was reluctant to allow such elections, fearing a communist victory.

The Role of the United States and the Failure of Reunification

The United States, motivated by Cold War concerns, played a crucial role in the post-Geneva political landscape in Vietnam. Fearing the spread of communism in Southeast Asia, the U.S. refused to sign the Geneva Accords and instead supported the establishment of a strong anti-communist government in the South.

In 1955, the staunchly anti-communist Ngo Dinh Diem, organized a referendum that deposed Boa Dai and ended the monarchy, with Diem becoming president of South Vietnam. Diem's regime, with American support, refused to hold the reunification elections, arguing that free and fair elections were impossible in the communist-controlled North.

This led to a prolonged period of instability and tension between North and South Vietnam. The division at the 17th parallel became more than just a temporary separation; it crystallized into a deep political and ideological divide that would shape the future of Vietnam. Diem's authoritarian rule and policies alienated many South Vietnamese, leading to internal dissent and the emergence of the National Liberation Front (NLF), also known as the Viet Cong, a communist-led insurgency in the South supported by the North.

The Geneva Accords and the Prelude to the Vietnam War

The Geneva Accords ultimately failed to achieve the peaceful reunification of Vietnam. The division between North and South, fueled by Cold War dynamics, set the stage for further conflict. As tensions escalated, both the North and South prepared for an inevitable confrontation. The United States increased its involvement in Vietnam, providing military and financial support to the South Vietnamese government, while the North, led by Ho Chi Minh, continued to pursue its goal of reunification under communist rule.

U.S. Marines during operation in Hue City, 1968

By the early 1960s, the situation in Vietnam had reached a boiling point, with the U.S. escalating its involvement to counter the perceived threat of communism. The inability of the Geneva Accords to provide a lasting solution to the division of Vietnam led directly to the outbreak of the Vietnam War, a conflict that would have profound and lasting consequences for Vietnam, the United States, and the world.

2. THE COLD WAR AND U.S. INVOLVEMENT

The Cold War was a massive global power struggle that defined much of the 20th century. It wasn't about direct military battles but more about an intense competition between two ideologies: capitalism and democracy, led by the United States, and communism, championed by the Soviet Union. The Vietnam War became a major hotspot in this larger conflict because the U.S. was determined to stop the spread of communism. This fear was tied to something called the "Domino Theory" - the idea that if one country in Southeast Asia fell to communism, the others around it would quickly follow.

To really understand why the U.S. got involved in Vietnam, we have to look at the broader Cold War tensions and how deeply the Domino Theory influenced American leaders.

I. The Struggle Between Communism and Capitalism

After World War II, the alliance between the United States and the Soviet Union quickly dissolved into a battle of ideological differences, of democracy and capitalism vs communism. As the two superpowers emerged, they sought to expand their influence worldwide, leading to a struggle for control over strategic regions. This "cold" war was characterized by political and military pressure, propaganda, espionage, and economic competition, rather than direct battles between the two superpowers.

One of the primary concerns of the United States was the spread of communism. American leaders believed that communism posed a direct threat to democracy, individual rights, and the free-market system. Under this mindset, the U.S. developed a foreign policy based on "containment," a strategy aimed at preventing the spread of communism beyond countries that were already under Soviet influence. The containment policy was articulated in what became known as the "Truman Doctrine" in 1947. Named after President Harry Truman, it committed the U.S. to support countries resisting communist takeover, beginning with Greece and Turkey, and marked the start of active American efforts to counter Soviet influence globally.

By the 1950s, Asia had become a major battleground in the Cold War. In 1949, the communists, led by Mao Zedong, gained control of China, establishing the People's Republic of China. This victory was a blow to the United States, which had supported the opposing Nationalist forces, and signaled to American leaders that communism was gaining a foothold in Asia.

Soon after, in 1950, the Korean War broke out, further highlighting the intensity of Cold War competition in the region. The Korean War ended in a stalemate in 1953, with the country divided into communist North Korea and non-communist South Korea, a situation that still exists today. This division reinforced the U.S. determination to prevent similar outcomes in other Asian nations.

With its own long history of resistance against foreign control, Vietnam found itself caught in the crosshairs of Cold War tensions. As we've already seen, the Geneva Accords of 1954 temporarily divided Vietnam at the 17th parallel, with Ho Chi Minh's communist government in the North and a U.S.-backed government in the South.

The U.S. government saw the division of Vietnam as an opportunity to contain communism in Southeast Asia. Leaders in Washington were concerned that if Ho Chi Minh and his communist allies were allowed to unite Vietnam under communist rule, it could set a precedent for other countries in the region to adopt communism as well. These fears were exacerbated by the fact that Vietnam was geographically close to several other vulnerable countries, including Laos, Cambodia, Thailand, and Indonesia. American leaders believed that if communism took hold in Vietnam, these other nations could be the next dominoes to fall.

II.◻The Domino Theory: The Fear of Communism Spreading Across Southeast Asia

The idea that communism could spread from one country to its neighbors, like falling dominoes, became known as the "Domino Theory." This theory was central to American Cold War strategy, especially in Southeast Asia. The term was first introduced by President Dwight D. Eisenhower in 1954, shortly after the French were defeated in Vietnam. In a press conference, Eisenhower explained that the loss of Vietnam to communism could trigger a chain reaction across the region, with one country after another "falling" to communism. The Domino Theory was rooted in a fear of communism's appeal to impoverished or colonized populations. American leaders worried that if one country successfully adopted communism, others might follow, seeing it as a viable path to independence and prosperity.

The Domino Theory was based on both ideological concerns and strategic calculations. Ideologically, the U.S. saw communism as antithetical to its values of individual freedom and democracy. Strategically, the theory suggested that a single country's shift to communism would weaken the U.S. position in Asia, which could threaten American allies and interests. If the U.S. did not act to prevent Vietnam from becoming communist, leaders feared that other nations in the region, particularly U.S. allies, would question America's commitment to their security. This could undermine American influence and allow the Soviet Union and China to expand their own.

In Southeast Asia, the U.S. government worked to reinforce its alliances and increase its support for anti-communist governments. The U.S. strengthened its ties with countries such as Thailand and the Philippines, seeing them as critical partners in the effort to resist communism. Additionally, American officials began to support South Vietnam as it represented not only a strategic buffer but also a symbol of resistance to communism.

U.S. Marines in Vietnam

In practice, the Domino Theory led the U.S. to invest significant resources in supporting anti-communist governments, regardless of their political practices or popular support. American leaders often assumed that any government opposing communism, even authoritarian regimes, was preferable to allowing communists to gain power.

This approach sometimes led the U.S. to support leaders who were unpopular or repressive, which undermined the very values of democracy and freedom that America claimed to champion. In South Vietnam, for example, the U.S. provided support to President Ngo Dinh Diem, whose leadership was marked by corruption, authoritarianism, and religious favoritism. Diem's government struggled to win support from the Vietnamese population, many of whom viewed him as a puppet of the United States.

The Domino Theory continued to influence American involvement in Vietnam as the conflict escalated. After the Gulf of Tonkin incident in 1964, when North Vietnamese forces reportedly attacked U.S. naval vessels, President Lyndon B. Johnson used the incident to justify increased American military intervention. With Congress's approval, Johnson ordered a massive buildup of U.S. troops in Vietnam, hoping to prevent the communist North from taking over the South. The conflict transformed from a regional struggle into a full-scale war involving hundreds of thousands of American soldiers and resulting in a significant loss of life and resources on both sides.

Over time, however, the validity of the Domino Theory came into question. While the theory assumed that communism would spread uniformly across Asia, it failed to account for the diversity of cultures, histories, and political dynamics in the region. It became evident that not all nations were likely to adopt communism simply because a neighboring country did. For example, while Laos and Cambodia experienced communist takeovers, other nations in Southeast Asia, such as Thailand, Malaysia, and Indonesia, maintained their independence and resisted communist influence.

The Domino Theory may have oversimplified the complexities of Southeast Asia's political landscape, leading to a costly and ultimately unsuccessful American intervention. However, during the Cold War, the theory resonated deeply with American leaders, who were genuinely concerned about the global spread of communism and the possibility of Soviet and Chinese dominance. This fear drove the United States to make significant sacrifices to prevent what they saw as a catastrophic outcome.

The Cold War rivalry between the United States and the Soviet Union provided the ideological backdrop for the Vietnam War. The U.S. commitment to containing communism, led American leaders to view Vietnam as a critical battleground in the global struggle between communism and capitalism. While the Domino Theory reflected genuine concerns, it also led to miscalculations about the nature of the conflict in Vietnam and the motivations of the Vietnamese people.

The Vietnam War, initially viewed by the United States as a limited engagement aimed, quickly escalated into one of the most intense and prolonged military conflicts in American history. The road to full U.S. involvement began with a relatively modest commitment of military advisors and financial support, evolving into a major military campaign with hundreds of thousands of American troops deployed in Vietnam. This escalation was marked by a combination of Cold War anxiety, misjudgements, and events that dramatically increased U.S. commitment to South Vietnam's defence.

U.S. Marines loading artillery rounds

To understand how the United States became so deeply entangled in Vietnam, we must look first at the initial phases of U.S. support, beginning in the 1950s with limited assistance and growing into full military engagement by the early 1960s, culminating in the Gulf of Tonkin Incident, which would serve as the tipping point for American escalation.

III. Early U.S. Support: Advisors and Limited Involvement in the 1950s

The United States initially provided financial and logistical support to the French in their attempt to reassert control over Vietnam during the First Indochina War (1946–1954). However, when the French were defeated at Dien Bien Phu in 1954, the Geneva Accords were established, and Vietnam was divided at the 17th parallel. With fears of a communist takeover, American involvement in South Vietnam deepened.

President Dwight D. Eisenhower began providing direct support to the South Vietnamese, despite President Diem's controversial and often authoritarian rule. In 1955, the United States established the Military Assistance Advisory Group (MAAG) in Vietnam, which consisted of U.S. military advisors who would train the South Vietnamese army (ARVN). However, the role of these advisors was limited, as the U.S. was hesitant to commit combat troops directly.

Civilian irregular defence trainee, firing M79 Grenade Launcher

Despite the United States' increasing support, the South Vietnamese government struggled with internal instability and resistance from communist forces within South Vietnam, known as the Viet Cong. Diem's leadership faced numerous challenges, including his alienation of Buddhists and his inability to gain the trust of many South Vietnamese. This internal discord created opportunities for the Viet Cong to expand their influence, leading to rising violence and instability.

Escalation of U.S. Involvement in the Early 1960s

In 1961, as John F. Kennedy assumed the presidency, he inherited the growing problem of communist insurgency in South Vietnam. Kennedy believed that the United States needed to counter communist expansion. The Kennedy administration increased both financial aid and military advisors in South Vietnam, growing from around 700 advisors in 1960 to more than 16,000 by 1963. These advisors played a key role in training and assisting South Vietnamese forces, although they were officially limited to a non-combat role.

Kennedy's policy reflected a Cold War strategy of "flexible response," which sought to contain communism through a variety of means, rather than relying solely on nuclear deterrence. In Vietnam, this meant an expanded commitment to counter-insurgency efforts, which involved training the ARVN (Army of the Republic of Vietnam) and working on pacification programs to win the support of the rural population. The United States also introduced the Green Berets, to engage in covert operations aimed at weakening the Viet Cong.

Despite these efforts, the South Vietnamese government continued to face major difficulties. Diem's administration was increasingly viewed as corrupt and out of touch with the needs of ordinary Vietnamese citizens. In 1963, after a series of Buddhist protests and violent crackdowns by Diem's government, the U.S. tacitly supported a coup by South Vietnamese generals, resulting in Diem's assassination. However, instead of bringing stability, this coup led to political chaos, as successive governments struggled to maintain order. The weakening of South Vietnam's leadership structure left the country even more vulnerable to communist influence, prompting further U.S. involvement.

By the time Lyndon B. Johnson took office following Kennedy's assassination in 1963, the situation in Vietnam had worsened. Johnson was initially reluctant to escalate U.S. involvement, but he felt increasing pressure from military advisors and policymakers who argued that a stronger stance was necessary. This period of uncertainty would come to an end with the Gulf of Tonkin Incident in 1964, a pivotal event that transformed the U.S. commitment to Vietnam.

IV.◻The Gulf of Tonkin Incident: The Catalyst for Full-Scale Escalation

On August 2nd, 1964, the USS Maddox, a U.S. Navy destroyer, was conducting an intelligence-gathering mission in the Gulf of Tonkin, off the coast of North Vietnam. The Maddox came under attack by North Vietnamese torpedo boats. The ship managed to escape without significant damage, and the incident was reported back to Washington. President Johnson and his advisors viewed this attack as an act of aggression by North Vietnam, though the specifics of the incident were somewhat unclear.

Two days later, on August 4th, the USS Maddox and another U.S. destroyer, the USS Turner Joy, reported a second attack by North Vietnamese forces. This second attack, however, remains highly controversial, as later investigations cast doubt on whether it actually occurred. Some reports suggest that poor weather conditions and faulty radar equipment may have led to false alarms, with no actual engagement by North Vietnamese forces. Nevertheless, the Johnson administration presented the incident as a clear act of aggression, using it as grounds for a stronger response.

In the immediate aftermath of the reported attacks, President Johnson addressed the American public, describing the events as an unprovoked assault by North Vietnam. He used this as a basis to seek authorization from Congress to take further military action in Vietnam. On August 7th, 1964, Congress passed the Gulf of Tonkin Resolution with overwhelming support, granting Johnson the authority to use "all necessary measures" to repel armed attacks against U.S. forces and prevent further aggression.

The Gulf of Tonkin Resolution effectively gave Johnson a blank check to escalate U.S. military involvement in Vietnam without a formal declaration of war. This resolution marked a turning point in American involvement, transforming what had been primarily an advisory and support role into a full-scale military engagement. Shortly afterward, Johnson ordered airstrikes against North Vietnamese targets, and by 1965, he had committed tens of thousands of U.S. troops to combat in Vietnam.

Consequences of the Gulf of Tonkin Incident and the Escalation of the War

The Gulf of Tonkin Incident and the subsequent resolution drastically changed the nature of the U.S. involvement in Vietnam. Johnson's decision to deploy ground troops and increase bombing campaigns signaled a commitment to a sustained military effort aimed at defeating the Viet Cong and North Vietnamese forces. It would lead to the deployment of more than 500,000 American troops by the late 1960s, transforming Vietnam into one of the largest military undertakings in American history.

However, as U.S. involvement intensified, the realities of the Vietnam War became increasingly grim. American forces faced a determined enemy in the North Vietnamese Army and the Viet Cong, who used guerrilla warfare tactics, making conventional military superiority difficult to translate into lasting success. The dense jungles, unfamiliar terrain, and lack of clear battle lines meant that U.S. forces were often engaged in protracted and costly battles without decisive victories.

Marine With Viet Cong Activist

The Gulf of Tonkin Incident and Johnson's subsequent escalation began to spark significant public debate and protest within the United States. As American casualties mounted and the financial costs of the war grew, the American public began to question the necessity and morality of the U.S. presence in Vietnam. The escalation also eroded trust in government leaders, particularly as doubts emerged about the validity of the Gulf of Tonkin Incident itself.

In the end, the Gulf of Tonkin Incident represented more than just a single event; it was a catalyst that led the United States into a costly and divisive conflict. The incident and its aftermath reflect the complexity of Cold War-era decision-making, where the fear of communist expansion, fueled by the Domino Theory, often led to actions with far-reaching consequences. The Gulf of Tonkin Resolution provided the legal framework for what would become a prolonged and difficult conflict, illustrating how a combination of miscommunication, misinterpretation, and ideological zeal can transform a limited engagement into a full-scale war.

3. A WAR OF IDEOLOGIES – WHO WAS INVOLVED

The Vietnam War was not just a localized conflict between two opposing forces but also a global struggle between competing ideologies - communism and capitalism - on the world stage. Let's take a look at the various forces and countries involved.

I. *The Viet Cong and North Vietnamese Army*

The Viet Cong (VC) and the North Vietnamese Army (NVA) were the primary forces fighting for the unification of Vietnam under a communist government. The Viet Cong, also known as the National Front for the Liberation of South Vietnam (NLF), was a revolutionary group consisting largely of southern Vietnamese peasants and civilians who resisted the government of South Vietnam. Initially, the Viet Cong were organized as a guerrilla force, conducting hit-and-run tactics, ambushes, and sabotage operations. Over time, they grew into a formidable force, receiving training and logistical support from the North.

A Viet Cong officer

The NVA, based in North Vietnam, was the conventional military force of the communist government led by Ho Chi Minh. Unlike the Viet Cong, the NVA consisted of regular soldiers who were organized into units and trained in conventional warfare. The NVA was responsible for large-scale offensives and had more substantial firepower, including tanks, artillery, and advanced weaponry provided by the Soviet Union and China. Their strategy was to fight both a conventional and unconventional war, utilizing the difficult terrain of Vietnam, including jungles and mountains, to their advantage.

Commanders and Generals of the Viet Cong and NVA

1. Ho Chi Minh

Role: President of North Vietnam and figurehead of the communist movement.

Significance: While not a direct military commander, Ho Chi Minh was the ideological leader and symbol of Vietnamese independence and unification. His leadership inspired the NVA and VC forces.

2. General Võ Nguyên Giáp

Role: Commander-in-Chief of the North Vietnamese Army.

Notable Achievements:

- Architect of the Tet Offensive (1968) and major campaigns like the Dien Bien Phu victory against the French in 1954.

- Mastermind of guerrilla warfare and conventional military strategies, emphasizing resilience and long-term attrition to wear down the enemy.

Legacy: Recognized as one of the greatest military strategists of the 20th century.

3. Lê Duẩn

Role: General Secretary of the Communist Party of Vietnam and de facto leader of North Vietnam during the war.

Significance: Although not a military commander, Lê Duẩn played a key role in shaping the overall strategy of the war, emphasizing unification through military means.

4. Nguyễn Chí Thanh

Role: Senior NVA general and commander of communist forces in South Vietnam (early in the war).

Notable Contributions:

- Advocated for aggressive large-scale battles to weaken U.S. forces.

- Helped organize the Viet Cong into a more effective fighting force before his death in 1967.

5. Phạm Văn Đồng

Role: Political leader and North Vietnamese Prime Minister.

Significance: Collaborated closely with military leaders to align political objectives with military strategies.

6. Trần Văn Trà

Role: Commander of the Viet Cong's B2 Front, responsible for operations in southern Vietnam, including the Mekong Delta and Saigon region.

Notable Achievements:

- Played a major role in planning and executing the Tet Offensive (1968).
- Coordinated post-Tet operations leading to the eventual capture of Saigon in 1975.

7. Văn Tiến Dũng

Role: Chief of Staff of the NVA and later its overall commander.

Notable Achievements:

- Planned and led the Ho Chi Minh Campaign (1975), the final offensive that captured Saigon and ended the war.
- Key figure in transitioning from guerrilla tactics to large-scale conventional warfare.

8. Nguyễn Hữu An

Role: NVA general and commander in several major battles.

Notable Contributions:

Played a crucial role in the Battle of Ia Drang (1965), the first major engagement between U.S. and NVA forces.

Known for his effective use of maneuver warfare and coordination in large-scale battles.

Tactics

Tactically, the Viet Cong and NVA relied heavily on guerrilla warfare. They used the extensive network of tunnels in the Cu Chi region, for instance, to hide from airstrikes and launch surprise attacks. They also made use of booby traps, land mines, and improvised explosive devices (IEDs) to inflict casualties on the invading forces, often using their knowledge of the local terrain to elude detection.

One of the key strengths of the Viet Cong and NVA was their ability to endure the harsh conditions of the war. They were accustomed to fighting in the dense jungles and rice paddies of Vietnam, where the American military's superior firepower was less effective. The North Vietnamese forces maintained a strong sense of ideological commitment. They fought not only to defeat an external enemy but also to liberate their country from what they saw as a corrupt and oppressive regime imposed by the United States.

II. The U.S. and the Army of the Republic of Vietnam (ARVN)

The United States and its allies, including South Korea, Australia, and Thailand, supported the government of South Vietnam. The Army of the Republic of Vietnam (ARVN) was created after the division of Vietnam into North and South in 1954 and became the military force of the South Vietnamese Republic. The ARVN was tasked with defending the South from both internal insurgencies, like the Viet Cong, and external threats from North Vietnam.

Commanders and Generals of the ARVN

1. General Nguyễn Khánh

Role: ARVN General and South Vietnam's head of state (1964–1965).

Significance:

- Played a major role in the 1963 coup that overthrew President Ngô Đình Diệm.

- Faced criticism for political instability during his tenure as leader of South Vietnam.

- Known for frequent reshuffling of ARVN leadership, which weakened the military's effectiveness.

2. General Cao Văn Viên

Role: Chief of the Joint General Staff of the ARVN (1965–1975).

Notable Achievements:

- Held the highest-ranking military position in South Vietnam for most of the war.

- Worked closely with U.S. advisors to modernize the ARVN and coordinate military operations.

- Respected for his professionalism and apolitical stance.

Legacy: Evacuated to the United States in 1975, where he authored works on ARVN's history.

3. General Dương Văn Minh

Role: ARVN General and later President of South Vietnam.

Significance:

- Key figure in the 1963 coup against President Ngô Đình Diệm.

- Known as "Big Minh," he briefly led South Vietnam as president during the country's collapse in April 1975.

- Ordered the surrender of South Vietnam to North Vietnam to avoid further bloodshed.

4. General Ngô Quang Trưởng

Role: Commander of ARVN's IV Corps and later I Corps.

Notable Achievements:

- Regarded as one of ARVN's most competent and effective generals.
- Successfully led the defense of the Mekong Delta in the early 1970s.
- Played a key role during the Easter Offensive (1972), where he defended Hue and Da Nang against NVA attacks.

5. General Lê Nguyên Khang

Role: Commander of the ARVN Marines.

- Notable Achievements:
- Led the ARVN Marine Corps with distinction in some of the war's toughest battles.
- Worked closely with U.S. Marine advisors, earning respect from American counterparts.

6. General Nguyễn Văn Toàn

Role: Commander of II Corps and IV Corps at different times during the war.

Significance:

- Oversaw ARVN operations in the Central Highlands, a strategically vital region.
- Criticized for his leadership during the Battle of Ban Me Thuot (1975), which led to the loss of the Central Highlands.

7. General Trần Văn Minh

Role: Commander of the Air Force of the Republic of Vietnam (RVNAF).

Significance:

- Led South Vietnam's air force, the largest and most advanced in Southeast Asia during the war.

- Played a key role in air support operations alongside U.S. forces.

8. General Phạm Văn Phú

Role: Commander of II Corps (Central Highlands).

Notable Contributions:

- Fought during the critical Battle of Kontum (1972), successfully repelling NVA attacks.

- Commanded during the disastrous Battle of Ban Me Thuot (1975), which marked the beginning of South Vietnam's collapse.

9. General Trần Thiện Khiêm

Role: ARVN General and later Prime Minister of South Vietnam (1969–1975).

Significance:

- Played a major role in South Vietnam's political and military leadership.

- Helped stabilize the government during a turbulent period.

The United States played a central role in the development and operation of the ARVN, providing military training, equipment, and financial support. American advisors and trainers helped turn the ARVN into a more professional fighting force, but the challenges they faced were significant. The ARVN struggled with internal corruption, political interference, and frequent leadership changes that undermined its cohesion and effectiveness. Moreover, the morale of ARVN soldiers was often low, particularly as the war dragged on, with many questioning the legitimacy of their government.

Despite these issues, the ARVN did achieve some successes. It fought in key battles, such as the Battle of Ap Bac in 1963, where the South Vietnamese forces successfully defended against a Viet Cong attack, and the Battle of Dong Ap Bia, known as Hamburger Hill, in 1969, where ARVN forces fought alongside U.S. troops to repel NVA forces. However, the ARVN's ability to defeat the Viet Cong and NVA remained limited. The guerrilla tactics used by the enemy were often more effective than the conventional strategies employed by the ARVN.

III. The Soviet Union and China

The Soviet Union and China played crucial roles in supporting the North Vietnamese forces. Both communist powers saw the Vietnam War as part of the larger ideological struggle against Western imperialism, particularly the United States. Their support included military aid, training, and financial resources.

The Soviet Union, under leaders Nikita Khrushchev and later Leonid Brezhnev, provided North Vietnam with advanced weaponry, including surface-to-air missiles, artillery, tanks, and fighter jets. Soviet training programs helped to professionalize the NVA, while its diplomatic support on the global stage helped legitimize the communist cause. The Soviet Union's involvement in Vietnam was part of its broader Cold War strategy to expand communist influence and counter U.S. efforts to contain it.

China, led by Mao Zedong, also contributed significant support to North Vietnam. China provided military aid, such as weapons, ammunition, and training for the Viet Cong. Despite ideological differences between China and the Soviet Union, both countries saw the Vietnam War as an opportunity to bolster their influence in Southeast Asia. China's support was critical in ensuring that North Vietnam had the resources needed to continue the war, especially when the U.S. escalated its involvement in the mid-1960s.

IV. The United States

The United States entered the Vietnam War under the pretext of stopping the spread of communism in Southeast Asia, as part of its containment strategy, which sought to prevent the domino effect of nations falling under communist rule. The U.S. began providing military assistance to South Vietnam in the late 1950s, but its direct involvement escalated following the Gulf of Tonkin incident in 1964, leading to the deployment of combat troops in 1965.

U.S. Generals

Several U.S. generals played significant roles in the Vietnam War, overseeing different phases of the conflict and various aspects of military strategy.

1.❏General Paul D. Harkins (1962–1964)

General Paul D. Harkins

Role: First commander of Military Assistance Command, Vietnam (MACV), the organization responsible for U.S. military operations in Vietnam.

Focus: Overseeing the early U.S. advisory role to the South Vietnamese military.

Challenges: Criticized for overly optimistic assessments of the South Vietnamese Army's (ARVN) performance.

2. General William C. Westmoreland (1964–1968)

Role: Commander of MACV during the critical escalation of U.S. involvement.

Strategy: Advocated for a strategy of attrition, using large-scale search-and-destroy missions and heavy reliance on firepower to weaken the North Vietnamese Army (NVA) and Viet Cong.

Notable Events:

- Oversaw major operations like the Battle of Ia Drang and the Tet Offensive (1968).

- His approach faced criticism for failing to adapt to guerrilla warfare tactics.

Legacy: Viewed as a polarizing figure; some praise his leadership under difficult circumstances, while others criticize his focus on body counts as a measure of success.

3. General Creighton W. Abrams (1968–1972)

Role: Replaced Westmoreland as commander of MACV.

Strategy: Shifted focus to Vietnamization, the process of building up South Vietnamese forces to take over combat roles as U.S. troops began withdrawing.

Notable Events:

- Oversaw the reduction of U.S. troop levels.

- Managed operations during the Cambodian Incursion (1970) and the Easter Offensive (1972).

Legacy: Credited with improving coordination with ARVN and shifting to more sustainable strategies.

4. General Frederick C. Weyand (1972–1973)

Role: Last U.S. commander of MACV before the Paris Peace Accords (1973).

Focus: Oversaw the final phase of U.S. involvement in the war, including the drawdown of American forces.

Legacy: Played a key role in transitioning responsibility to South Vietnamese forces.

Other Notable Figures:

Admiral Ulysses S. Grant Sharp: Commander of U.S. Pacific Command (PACOM), responsible for overall military operations in the Pacific, including Vietnam.

General Maxwell D. Taylor: Chairman of the Joint Chiefs of Staff (1962–1964) and later U.S. Ambassador to South Vietnam, heavily involved in shaping early U.S. policy in Vietnam.

General Earle G. Wheeler: Chairman of the Joint Chiefs of Staff during much of the war, coordinating military strategy at the highest level.

Strategies

The U.S. military employed a variety of strategies and tactics to combat the Viet Cong and the NVA. One of the most significant was the use of air power. The U.S. conducted extensive bombing campaigns, such as Operation Rolling Thunder and Operation Linebacker, which targeted North Vietnamese infrastructure, supply routes, and military bases. However, the bombing campaigns were often ineffective in halting the enemy's war effort and led to significant civilian casualties, further undermining U.S. support for the war.

Helicopters played a huge role. They gave U.S. forces the ability to move troops quickly, launch air assaults, and evacuate the wounded, which was essential in a war fought in dense jungles and tough terrain. The Huey helicopter, in particular, became an iconic image of the war, combining mobility and firepower in ways that transformed how battles were fought.

A controversial tactic was the use of Agent Orange, a powerful chemical sprayed to clear the jungle vegetation that gave the Viet Cong and NVA cover. While it was effective in exposing enemy positions, it left a devastating legacy. Agent Orange caused severe environmental damage and long-term health problems for both Vietnamese civilians and the U.S. soldiers who were exposed to it.

While the U.S. had superior technology, including advanced air power, artillery, and tanks, it struggled with the tactics of its enemies and the difficult terrain.

The Viet Cong's guerrilla tactics and intimate knowledge of the local terrain often negated American advantages. The war was marked by ambushes, booby traps, and asymmetric engagements that made it difficult for conventional military forces to succeed.

4. KEY EVENTS AND TIMELINE

When we think about the Vietnam War, we often remember the protests, fierce battles, and heavy losses. But the war unfolded in distinct phases that really shaped how things played out. One of the most crucial periods was from 1954 to 1968, when the North-South divide in Vietnam became clear, U.S. involvement ramped up, and a series of key events started to shift how Americans saw the war.

We've already touched on some of these events in earlier chapters, but they're included here again to give you a full picture of the timeline.

I.口1954-1960: The Seeds of Conflict

The roots of the Vietnam War can be traced to colonial struggles and ideological divides in the aftermath of World War II. The French, who had ruled Vietnam as part of French Indochina, faced resistance from Vietnamese nationalists, culminating in the First Indochina War (1946–1954) between French forces and the Viet Minh, a communist-led nationalist movement headed by Ho Chi Minh.

In 1954, the Geneva Accords were signed, establishing a ceasefire and temporarily dividing Vietnam at the 17th parallel into North and South Vietnam. The Geneva Accords were intended to be a temporary measure until nationwide elections could be held in 1956, but these elections never took place, deepening the division between North and South and sowing the seeds for future conflict.

In 1955, Diem assumed leadership in South Vietnam and established the Republic of Vietnam, declaring himself president after a questionable referendum. Diem's authoritarian rule alienated many, especially among South Vietnam's rural population and Buddhist communities. Despite his unpopularity, the United States continued to support Diem, viewing his government as a bulwark against communism in Southeast Asia. The division of Vietnam and the lack of political cohesion in the South set the stage for a prolonged ideological and military struggle.

II.口1961-1964: Escalation of U.S. Involvement

In 1961, as the Cold War intensified, President John F. Kennedy sought to increase support for South Vietnam. Kennedy's administration adopted a policy of counterinsurgency, deploying military advisors and providing training to the South Vietnamese army.

The belief was that South Vietnam could be fortified to resist the growing influence of the communist National Liberation Front (NLF), commonly known as the Viet Cong, a group of South Vietnamese communists supported by the North. This period saw a gradual escalation of U.S. involvement, as Kennedy believed that losing Vietnam to communism would have dire consequences for U.S. influence in Asia and the global struggle against communism.

The Battle of Ap Bac

The Battle of Ap Bac was an early and pivotal engagement, fought in the Mekong Delta of South Vietnam in January 1963. It marked one of the first major clashes between the Viet Cong (VC) and South Vietnamese forces, supported by U.S. military advisors. Although it was not a large-scale battle, it became a symbolic moment that exposed challenges for the South Vietnamese military and the U.S. strategy.

The South Vietnamese planned to encircle and destroy the Viet Cong forces, who were entrenched in Ap Bac. However, the operation quickly ran into trouble for a number of reasons:

- The Viet Cong had fortified positions and were better prepared than anticipated.

- South Vietnamese troops were hesitant to advance, despite their numerical and technological superiority.

- U.S. helicopters faced heavy fire from the Viet Cong, resulting in several being shot down - a significant blow to U.S. morale and strategy.

- The ARVN's armored vehicles struggled to navigate the muddy rice paddies, limiting their effectiveness.

After a day of fierce fighting, the South Vietnamese forces withdrew, leaving the battlefield to the Viet Cong. Despite inflicting casualties on the Viet Cong, the ARVN failed to achieve its objective, and the Viet Cong claimed victory.

The Battle of Ap Bac demonstrated the complexity of fighting in Vietnam and foreshadowed the challenges the U.S. would face as its involvement deepened. It showed that military hardware alone wouldn't guarantee victory against a determined and resourceful enemy.

Instability in South Vietnam

In 1963, the U.S. commitment to Diem's government took a troubling turn. Diem's harsh policies, including repression of political opponents and violent persecution of Buddhist communities, sparked widespread protests and increased resentment toward his rule. The situation escalated when Buddhist monks began self-immolating in protest, shocking the international community. Recognizing that Diem's regime was increasingly unpopular and unstable, the U.S. covertly supported a coup that led to his overthrow and assassination on November 2nd, 1963. This act created further political instability in South Vietnam, as a series of military and civilian governments struggled to establish control.

The tipping point for U.S. military involvement came in August 1964, when North Vietnamese forces allegedly attacked U.S. naval vessels in the Gulf of Tonkin. This incident, known as the Gulf of Tonkin Incident, led Congress to pass the Gulf of Tonkin Resolution, authorizing President Lyndon B. Johnson to take all necessary measures to repel armed attacks against U.S. forces and prevent further aggression. Although later investigations cast doubt on the accuracy of the initial reports of the incident, it became the catalyst for a significant escalation in U.S. involvement in Vietnam.

III.◻1965-1968: Escalation and Turning Points

By 1965, the Vietnam conflict had escalated from an advisory mission to a full-scale war. Johnson's administration approved Operation Rolling Thunder, a sustained bombing campaign against North Vietnam. Johnson authorized the deployment of ground troops, and in March 1965, the first U.S. combat units arrived in Vietnam. What had been an advisory mission now became a direct military engagement, with the U.S. committing hundreds of thousands of troops over the coming years.

Operation Rolling Thunder

Operation Rolling Thunder was a sustained bombing campaign, intended to weaken North Vietnam's capacity to wage war in the South. Despite its massive scale, the operation ultimately failed to achieve its goals, illustrating the limits of air power in a complex conflict.

The operation ran from March 2nd, 1965 to November 2nd, 1968. The U.S Airforce, Navy and Marine Corp flew over 300,000 sorties and dropped over 864,000 tons of bombs!

Targets included military bases, bridges, railroads, the Ho Chi Minh Trail and industrial facilities.

Despite this firepower, results were limited. While the bombing caused extensive damage and significant casualties, North Vietnam's resolve was not weakened. Supplies continued to flow through the Ho Chi Minh Trail, and support for the Viet Cong remained strong. Many civilians were killed or displaced due to the bombing. Villages, schools, and hospitals were sometimes hit, fueling anti-American sentiment in Vietnam and criticism abroad and intensified anti-war protests in the United States.

Operation Rolling Thunder remains one of the most controversial aspects of the Vietnam War. It showed the limits of air power in achieving political and military goals and demonstrated the challenges of fighting an asymmetric war against a determined adversary. The campaign's high cost in lives and resources ultimately contributed to growing doubts about U.S. strategy in Vietnam.

The Battle of Ia Drang

One of the first big clashes between U.S. and North Vietnamese forces happened in November 1965 at Ia Drang, in Vietnam's Central Highlands, a remote area marked by dense jungle and rugged terrain. The battle is often divided into two distinct phases, fought at two locations: Landing Zone (LZ) X-Ray and LZ Albany.

- **LZ X-Ray (November 14th – 16th, 1965):**

U.S. forces from the 1st Cavalry Division, using newly developed air mobility tactics with helicopters, landed at LZ X-Ray near the Chu Pong Massif, close to the Cambodian border. Their mission was to locate and engage NVA forces believed to be operating in the area. The battle quickly escalated into fierce close-quarters combat, as the outnumbered American troops faced a determined and well-coordinated NVA assault. Despite being heavily outnumbered, the U.S. forces used intensive artillery support, close air support, and helicopter resupply to hold their position and inflict heavy casualties on the enemy.

- **LZ Albany (November 17th, 1965):**

After the fighting at LZ X-Ray, U.S. forces began withdrawing toward another landing zone, LZ Albany. On the way, they were ambushed by NVA troops. The resulting battle was chaotic and devastating, with heavy casualties on both sides. The Americans suffered significant losses due to the element of surprise and the dense jungle, which hindered communication and maneuverability.

This battle was a major turning point because it showed just how intense and brutal the fighting would be. It was the first time U.S. troops, using helicopters for quick mobility, went head-to-head with the well-organized North Vietnamese Army (NVA). While the U.S. declared victory due to higher enemy casualties, the battle made it clear that this would be a long and deadly conflict. Both sides started to realize that traditional measures of success, like counting bodies, wouldn't be enough to bring the war to an end.

The Battle of Ia Drang was later immortalized in the book We Were Soldiers Once... and Young by Harold G. Moore, who commanded U.S. forces at LZ X-Ray, and journalist Joseph L. Galloway. Their account vividly captures the courage, chaos, and tragedy of the battle.

The Tet Offensive

The year 1968 marked a critical turning point in the Vietnam War. In January, the North Vietnamese and Viet Cong forces launched a coordinated series of surprise attacks known as the Tet Offensive (it occurred during Tet, the Vietnamese Lunar New Year holiday, which had traditionally been a time of truce).

The offensive is remembered as a pivotal moment in the Vietnam War. It showed just how determined the North Vietnamese forces were and revealed the limits of U.S. military power in such a complex political and cultural conflict. It also highlighted how much public perception and media coverage can influence the direction of modern warfare.

What Happened?

1.Surprise Attacks:

On January 30th – 31st, 1968, North Vietnamese and Viet Cong forces launched surprise attacks on over 100 cities, towns, and military bases across South Vietnam, including the capital, Saigon.

Key targets included the U.S. Embassy in Saigon, the ancient city of Hue, and major provincial capitals.

2.Fighting in Saigon:

In Saigon, attackers penetrated the grounds of the U.S. Embassy, sparking intense urban combat. While U.S. and South Vietnamese forces repelled the attackers, the imagery of the attack shook public confidence back in America.

ARVN Rangers defending Saigon, 1968

Battle of Hue:

The battle for the city of Hue lasted nearly a month and was one of the most intense of the war. North Vietnamese forces seized the city and held it for weeks, during which they executed thousands of suspected South Vietnamese collaborators.

3. Heavy Casualties:

The offensive resulted in massive casualties on both sides. Tens of thousands of North Vietnamese and Viet Cong troops were killed, while U.S. and South Vietnamese forces also suffered significant losses. Civilians were caught in the crossfire, and many were killed or displaced.

Why Was It Significant?

1. Psychological Impact:

Although the U.S. and South Vietnamese forces ultimately regained control of all the areas attacked, the offensive shattered the perception that the U.S. was winning the war.

The sheer scale and intensity of the attacks made it clear that North Vietnamese forces were far from defeated.

2. Media and Public Opinion:

Graphic news coverage of the fighting, particularly in Saigon and Hue, reached audiences in the U.S. and painted a grim picture of the war.

The Tet Offensive eroded public trust in the Johnson administration, which had been claiming that victory was near.

3. Strategic Outcomes:

Militarily, the offensive was a disaster for North Vietnam and the Viet Cong, who suffered heavy losses and lost all territory it had captured.

Politically, however, it was a success, as it turned American public opinion against the war and increased pressure to seek a negotiated settlement.

4. Political Fallout in the U.S.:

The Tet Offensive led President Lyndon B. Johnson to scale back escalation efforts, announcing that the bombing of North Vietnam would cease above the 20th parallel and placed a limit on U.S. troops in South Vietnam. Johnson also announced he would not seek re-election in 1968.

It marked a turning point where the U.S. began to shift from full-scale military engagement toward eventual withdrawal.

The My Lai Massacre

The My Lai Massacre on March 16th, 1968 added to the growing disillusionment with the war. U.S. soldiers from Charlie Company, led by Lieutenant William Calley, killed hundreds of unarmed Vietnamese civilians in the village of My Lai, including women, children, and elderly people. It's estimated that between 347 and 504 were killed.

The massacre was initially covered up but was later exposed, sparking outrage in the United States and internationally.

Lieutenant William Calley was the only person convicted. He was found guilty of murdering 22 villagers but served only three and a half years under house arrest after his life sentence was commuted.

The massacre became a symbol of the war's moral and strategic failures, highlighting issues like the dehumanization of the enemy, poor leadership, and lack of accountability. It fueled anti-war sentiment and increasing calls for accountability and an end to the war.

The Siege of Khe Sanh

In early 1968, U.S. forces also faced intense pressure at the Siege of Khe Sanh, a prolonged and bloody confrontation near the demilitarized zone (DMZ). Khe Sanh was located along Route 9, a key supply route, and was close to the Ho Chi Minh Trail, which the North Vietnamese used to move troops and supplies into South Vietnam.

The North Vietnamese sought to draw U.S. troops into a protracted battle, hoping to weaken American resolve. Around 20,000 – 30,000 NVA troops surrounded the base, and heavy shelling targeted the base's ammunition and fuel supplies.

A massive U.S. aerial bombardment campaign, codenamed Operation Niagara, was launched to destroy NVA positions around Khe Sanh. Over 100,000 tons of bombs were dropped, making it one of the most intense bombing campaigns of the war.

By April 1968, the North Vietnamese began withdrawing, possibly due to mounting losses and the inability to break U.S. defenses.

Although the U.S. ultimately held the base, the siege showed the high costs and limited gains of the war effort. The battle underscored the challenges of fighting a well-organized enemy willing to engage in lengthy, attritional warfare.

In July 1968, U.S. forces abandoned Khe Sanh, sparking debates over whether holding the base had been worth the cost.

☐ *DID YOU KNOW*

- The U.S. and Allies suffered 500 killed and over 2,500 wounded.

- For the North Vietnamese, there were between 10,000 – 15,000 killed.

Johnson's Decision Not to Seek Re-election

The events of 1968, especially the Tet Offensive and rising anti-war protests, had a profound impact on President Johnson's political future. By this point, public trust in the government was waning, and the war had become a divisive issue in American society. On March 31st, 1968, Johnson announced that he would not seek re-election, acknowledging the deep divisions caused by the war and signaling a shift in U.S. policy toward a de-escalation of the conflict. This decision marked a turning point in U.S. involvement in Vietnam, as the Johnson administration sought to find a way to negotiate an end to the war.

Let's now take a look at the period between 1969 and 1972 which marked a critical phase in the Vietnam War, with the U.S. shifting military responsibility to South Vietnam, the continuation of intense combat, and growing public opposition to the war in the United States.

IV.☐1969: Nixon Takes Office and Begins Vietnamization

In January 1969, Richard Nixon was inaugurated as the 37th President of the United States. His administration inherited the Vietnam War, a conflict that had already claimed tens of thousands of American lives and cost billions of dollars. Nixon's approach to the war marked a departure from the previous administration's escalation strategy. He introduced Vietnamization, a policy to reduce U.S. involvement by transferring military and logistical burdens to the South Vietnamese government, led by President Nguyen Van Thieu, who had been in power since 1965. Nixon believed that by bolstering the South Vietnamese military and shifting the fight to them, the U.S. could withdraw without appearing to abandon its allies. The idea was to "create the conditions for peace" by enabling the South Vietnamese forces to fight their own war, supported by U.S. air and artillery power when necessary.

While this plan resonated with American public sentiment, which was increasingly weary of the war, it was also a delicate balancing act. Nixon had to maintain enough U.S. military presence to prevent a collapse of the South Vietnamese regime while also keeping his promise to scale back American involvement. Despite these efforts, Vietnamization faced numerous challenges, including the South Vietnamese military's lack of resources, morale issues, and inadequate training.

V. 1970: Invasion of Cambodia and the Expansion of the War

One of the most controversial actions of Nixon's presidency occurred in 1970 when U.S. and South Vietnamese forces invaded Cambodia in an effort to disrupt North Vietnamese supply routes and sanctuaries in the country. The invasion of Cambodia, known as Operation Menu, was intended to target North Vietnamese Army (NVA) units operating along the Ho Chi Minh Trail, which passed through Cambodia.

The U.S. government justified the invasion as a necessary military action to weaken the North Vietnamese and protect South Vietnam. However, the move sparked outrage both domestically and internationally. Many saw the invasion as an expansion of the war, violating the neutrality of Cambodia and deepening U.S. involvement in Southeast Asia. The invasion led to widespread protests, especially on college campuses, with one of the most tragic events occurring at Kent State University in Ohio, where National Guard troops opened fire on students protesting against the invasion, killing four.

The invasion of Cambodia did not produce the desired results, and it further alienated the American public. Despite the operation's short-term military goals, it failed to decisively weaken the North Vietnamese or alter the strategic balance of the war.

VI. 1971: Pentagon Papers Leak and Growing Domestic Opposition

In 1971, a significant domestic event further eroded public trust in the U.S. government's handling of the war. The Pentagon Papers, a top-secret Department of Defense report detailing the U.S. government's activities in Vietnam from 1945 to 1967, were leaked to the press by former Pentagon official Daniel Ellsberg. The papers revealed that successive U.S. administrations had systematically misled the American public about the nature and progress of the war.

The papers exposed that U.S. leaders had misled Congress and the public about the true extent of the war, including secret bombings in Cambodia and Laos and plans to escalate the conflict even as they publicly spoke of de-escalation.

They revealed a long history of government deception regarding the war's objectives, strategies, and likelihood of success. They showed that many officials privately believed the war was unwinnable long before the American public was made aware.

The leak of the Pentagon Papers had a profound impact on American public opinion, sparking widespread disillusionment with the war and increasing anti-war activism.

For Nixon, the leak presented a major challenge. It not only undermined the credibility of the government but also intensified public protests. Anti-war demonstrations grew larger and more vocal, particularly as the U.S. continued to bomb North Vietnam and expand its military operations in Southeast Asia.

VII.◻1972: The Easter Offensive and Vietnamization's Limits

By 1972, the war was entering a crucial phase. The policy of Vietnamization faced its first major test when North Vietnam launched the Easter Offensive in March. The offensive, which was the largest North Vietnamese military action since the Tet Offensive of 1968, involved a series of attacks across South Vietnam.

North Vietnam aimed to capture significant territory in South Vietnam, weaken the South Vietnamese military, and force the U.S. to make concessions in peace talks in Paris.

The attack was launched on three main fronts:

- **Quảng Trị Province:** In the northernmost region, close to the Demilitarized Zone (DMZ).

- **Central Highlands:** Targeting the city of Kon Tum to cut South Vietnam in two.

- **Southern Region:** Focusing on Bình Long Province, near Saigon, to threaten the capital.

The North Vietnamese used large-scale conventional tactics, including tanks and artillery, marking a departure from their usual guerrilla warfare.

South Vietnamese forces, supported by U.S. air power, fought back fiercely, with intense battles over key cities like An Lộc and Quảng Trị.

Despite initial fears that the offensive would result in the collapse of South Vietnam, the South Vietnamese forces, with U.S. air support, managed to repel the attacks, although at a high cost. The Easter Offensive exposed the weaknesses of the South Vietnamese military, without American support, highlighting the challenges inherent in Vietnamization.

VIII.☐1972: The Christmas Bombing and Operation Linebacker

In response to the Easter Offensive and continued North Vietnamese aggression, Nixon authorized one of the most intense bombing campaigns of the war. From December 18th to December 29th, 1972, U.S. B-52 bombers conducted a massive bombing campaign known as Operation Linebacker II, commonly referred to as the Christmas Bombing. The goal was to force North Vietnam into negotiating more favorable terms during peace talks, and to inflict maximum damage on its infrastructure, including supply depots, transportation networks, and military installations in Hanoi and Haiphong.

Unlike earlier bombing campaigns (like Operation Rolling Thunder), Linebacker had fewer restrictions, allowing strikes against targets in and around Hanoi and Haiphong.

It heavily relied on advanced technology, including precision-guided "smart" bombs, for greater accuracy in targeting.

U.S. fighter jets and bombers, such as the F-4 Phantom and B-52 Stratofortress, played a central role. Navy aircraft carriers provided additional air support, and anti-aircraft suppression missions were conducted to neutralize North Vietnam's missile defenses.

Vietnam's key port, cutting off supplies from allies like China and the Soviet Union.

The bombing campaign was highly controversial, as it targeted heavily populated urban areas and caused significant civilian casualties. However, it did force the North Vietnamese to return to peace negotiations in Paris, signaling that both sides were seeking a way to end the conflict diplomatically.

IX.◻1973: The Paris Peace Accords and U.S. Withdrawal

On January 27th, 1973, the Paris Peace Accords were signed, officially ending direct U.S. involvement in the war. Under the terms of the agreement, the U.S. agreed to withdraw all combat forces from Vietnam, while both North and South Vietnam agreed to respect each other's territorial integrity. The North Vietnamese agreed to release American prisoners of war (POWs).

The Paris Peace Accords marked the formal end of U.S. combat involvement in Vietnam. South Vietnam was left to defend itself against the North, which had a far superior military in both resources and manpower. While the Paris Peace Accords were seen as a victory for Nixon in terms of achieving a diplomatic resolution and withdrawing U.S. troops, they did not bring peace to Vietnam.

In March 1973, the last U.S. combat troops left Vietnam, but the conflict continued between North and South Vietnam. The U.S. maintained a significant military and economic presence in the region through aid to South Vietnam, but the North was determined to reunify the country under its communist regime.

X.◻1975: The Fall of Saigon and the End of the War

In 1975, North Vietnamese forces launched a final offensive against South Vietnam. Cities such as Hue and Da Nang fell quickly, with South Vietnamese forces retreating in disarray.

By late April, North Vietnamese troops encircled Saigon. The South Vietnamese President Nguyễn Văn Thiệu resigned and fled the country, leaving a government in chaos.

As North Vietnamese forces closed in, the U.S. launched Operation Frequent Wind, the largest helicopter evacuation in history. Thousands of American personnel, South Vietnamese officials, and their families were airlifted to safety. Despite these efforts, many South Vietnamese who had worked with the U.S. were left behind, facing persecution under the new regime.

The Fall of Saigon on April 30th, 1975, marked the end of the war. North Vietnamese forces captured the capital of South Vietnam, Saigon, and the country was officially reunified under communist control.

Millions of South Vietnamese fled the country in the years following the fall, often risking their lives as "boat people" to escape persecution. Those who remained faced re-education camps, where many endured harsh treatment under the new communist government.

Vietnam was formally reunified as the Socialist Republic of Vietnam in July 1976, with Hanoi as its capital.

The U.S. had failed to prevent the collapse of South Vietnam, and the war's end marked a tragic chapter in American history. The U.S. withdrawal did not lead to peace in Vietnam; instead, it resulted in the establishment of the Socialist Republic of Vietnam under the control of Ho Chi Minh's communist government.

5. THE WAR IN NUMBERS

To understand the scale of the Vietnam War, we should look at numbers behind the armies, the civilians affected, and the human cost in both lives and sacrifices.

I. *American Forces in Vietnam*

- 2,709,918 American men and women served in Vietnam, representing about 9.7% of their generation.

- The size of U.S. forces peaked in April 1969, with 543,400 American soldiers.

- The average age of American soldiers in Vietnam was just 19!

- In total, around 1.9 million American men were conscripted or drafted during the war years, although not all of them served in Vietnam.

- Two thirds of those who served in Vietnam were volunteers.

- Of those who were drafted, approximately 648,500 ultimately served in Vietnam itself.

Despite the draft, a significant portion of American troops in Vietnam were volunteers, showing the strong anti-communist sentiment that motivated many young Americans to enlist, believing that they were taking part in a vital cause, defending freedom and democracy abroad. However, not all felt the same way; more than 125,000 Americans fled to Canada to avoid the draft, a significant demonstration of opposition to both conscription and the war itself.

II. *South Vietnam's Army: The ARVN*

- The Army of the Republic of Vietnam (ARVN), initially had approximately 150,000 troops.

- By the end of the war in 1975, the ARVN had grown to over one million soldiers. This growth was made possible through both local recruitment and extensive American support, including training, equipment, and financial aid.

III. North Vietnamese and Viet Cong Forces

- By 1966, the combined forces of the People's Army of Vietnam (PAVN) and the Viet Cong (VC) numbered approximately 690,000 troops.

Unlike the ARVN, which was heavily dependent on American assistance, the North Vietnamese forces operated with significant autonomy, supported primarily by the Soviet Union and China.

IV. Civilian and Military Casualties

The Vietnam War was devastating in terms of human cost, not only for the military personnel involved but also for civilians caught in the conflict.

- Civilian casualties in Vietnam, as well as in neighboring Cambodia and Laos, are estimated to be around 2 million, although exact numbers vary.

This figure reflects the intense violence and widespread destruction that affected entire villages and cities, often with tragic consequences for non-combatants. Airstrikes, artillery shelling, and the use of chemical agents like Agent Orange contributed to the civilian toll, leaving behind a legacy of suffering and environmental damage.

- Military casualties were also staggering. Between 1.1 million and 1.6 million North Vietnamese soldiers and Viet Cong fighters lost their lives during the conflict.

- On the South Vietnamese side, the ARVN suffered up to 250,000 military deaths.

- For American forces suffered 58,220 killed, with countless others wounded or psychologically scarred by their experiences.

- Other countries also suffered losses: South Korea lost 5,099 troops, Australia 523, and Thailand 351, underscoring the international nature of the conflict and the far-reaching impacts it had on soldiers from various nations.

V. American Casualty Statistics and the Human Dimension

The human cost of the Vietnam War is highlighted by the personal stories and statistics surrounding American casualties.

The average age of American soldiers killed in action was just 23.1 years.

- 61% of those killed were under 21 years old!

- Five Americans killed were just 16 years old, and one, Dan Bullock, was just 15! Bullock's case is particularly tragic; he enlisted under a falsified birth certificate that listed him as 18, demonstrating the lengths some young men would go to serve.

- One out of every 10 Americans who served in Vietnam was a casualty.

- The first American casualty was James Davis, in 1961. He was with the 509th Radio Research Station. Davis Station in Saigon was named after him.

- 1,448 American soldiers lost their lives on their last day of service in Vietnam, a reminder of the randomness and unpredictability of survival in combat.

- The toll on families was profound - 31 sets of U.S. brothers perished in Vietnam.

- 304,000 soldiers were wounded, with amputations or crippling wounds 300 percent higher than in World War II.

- The number of American soldiers who remain missing in action (MIA) as of 2022 stands at 1,244, leaving unresolved grief for their families and loved ones who continue to search for closure.

The helicopter war in Vietnam was another stark example of the risks soldiers faced. Helicopters were essential for troop transport, medical evacuation, and combat operations, but they also exposed their crews to extreme danger.

- Approximately 10% of American casualties in Vietnam were helicopter crew members, including door gunners whose role was especially perilous.

- 2 weeks...this was the average lifespan of a door gunner on a UH-1 "Huey" helicopter in Vietnam, a sobering reflection on the high-risk nature of this position and the vulnerability of those involved in air combat.

VI. Prisoners of War (POWs): Stories of Resilience and Survival

One of the most harrowing aspects of the Vietnam War was the experience of American soldiers captured and held as prisoners of war. These men endured extreme conditions, including physical abuse, isolation, and psychological torment, often for years.

- 766 Americans are known to have been prisoners of war. Of this number, 114 died during captivity.

- Torture was common and the Geneva Convention was not followed, as the North Vietnamese claimed the Americans were political criminals, not prisoners of war.

- The longest-held American POW in history, and the first to be taken prisoner in Vietnam, was Floyd Thompson, who was captured in 1964 and remained in captivity for nearly nine years (3,278 days!) until his release in 1973.

- Thompson's experience of resilience and endurance under unimaginable conditions is emblematic of the hardships faced by American POWs in Vietnam. Subjected to brutal treatment, starvation, and lack of medical care, many POWs returned with profound physical and psychological scars that would affect them for the rest of their lives.

- Another well-known POW was John McCain III, who later became a U.S. Senator and the 2008 Republican presidential nominee. McCain was held as a POW for over four years after being shot down during a bombing mission over Hanoi.

Like many other POWs, McCain experienced beatings, torture, and solitary confinement. His survival and subsequent public service underscored the profound impact of the war on those who served and sacrificed, and his story became symbolic of the resilience and dedication of American servicemen who endured captivity in Vietnam.

❏ *DID YOU KNOW*

- In 1973, the first 591 U.S. POWs were repatriated as part of Operation Homecoming.

- POWs were held in 13 prisons and camps in North Vietnam, including the notorious Hỏa Lò Prison, also known as the "Hanoi Hilton". Other POWs were held in South Vietnam, Cambodia, Laos, and China.

- American POWs gave nicknames to many of the camps, including Alcatrez, Briarpatch, the Zoo, and Dogpatch.

The goal of torturing and beating American prisoners wasn't really to gather military secrets, but to force them into making statements that criticized U.S. policies, which the North Vietnamese could then use for propaganda purposes. In 1966, Commander Jeremiah Denton, a captured Navy pilot, was forced to appear at a televised press conference, where he famously blinked the word "torture" with his eyes in Morse code, confirming suspicions of mistreatment..

The harsh environment and hostile population made escaped difficult, although some POWs still tried. Navy Lt. George Coker and USAF Capt. George McKnight escaped from "Dirty Bird" in Hanoi, and made it 15 miles down the Red River before being recaptured.

Hanoi Hilton POW camp

An escape attempt in May 1969 had horrific consequences for POWs. Air Force captains John Dramesi and Edwin Atterberry escaped from the "Zoo Annex" but only made a few miles before being captured. They had made clothing and props to blend in with the native population, and the prison authorities were furious that the Americans had been able to plan such a complex operation. This led to the most brutal and sustained episode of criminal inhumanity during the war. For two weeks, POWs on the "escape committee" who had helped Dramesi and Atterberry were tortured for details. The North Vietnamese murdered Atterberry by beating him to death, and they flogged Dramesi with fan belts for 38 straight days. They allowed him no sleep (he was forced to sit on a small stool the whole time), they beat him savagely, and alternately tied him in tight ropes or restrained him in irons as he was forced to write and tape apologies.

U.S. Former POWs returning home

VII.▢Honors: Recognizing Bravery and Sacrifice

The Vietnam War was a conflict that tested the bravery and resilience of those who served, and many American soldiers displayed acts of exceptional courage.

▢ *DID YOU KNOW*

- 244 soldiers were awarded the Medal of Honor, the United States' highest military award for valor.

These recipients exemplified heroism and selflessness, often risking their own lives to save others or complete their missions under enemy fire. Medal of Honor recipients from the Vietnam War represent a wide range of roles and backgrounds, from infantry soldiers and helicopter pilots to medics who risked everything to save the lives of their comrades.

VIII.▢Technology: Helicopters, Napalm, and Unexploded Ordnance

The Vietnam War was marked by significant advancements in military technology, much of which played a central role in combat strategy and operations. Among the most iconic elements was the widespread use of helicopters, which became a symbol of the war itself.

◻ *DID YOU KNOW*

- The U.S. deployed over 12,000 helicopters in Vietnam

- There was a cumulative total of more than 10 million flight hours.

- The average infantryman in Vietnam saw about 240 days of combat in one year thanks to the mobility of the helicopter.

- MEDEVAC helicopters flew nearly 500,000 missions. Over 900,000 patients were airlifted (nearly half were American).

- The average time lapse between wounding to hospitalization was less than one hour.

Helicopters such as the UH-1 "Huey" became essential for troop movement, medical evacuation, and close air support. However, the intense use of helicopters also exposed crew members to significant danger, and thousands of American servicemen lost their lives in helicopter-related incidents.

U.S. UH-1 "Huey"

Napalm was another infamous aspect of the Vietnam War's technology.

◻ ***DID YOU KNOW***

- U.S Between 1963 and 1973, the U.S. military dropped approximately 388,000 tons of napalm on Vietnam.

This jellied gasoline burned at temperatures exceeding 2,000 degrees Fahrenheit, causing devastating injuries and long-lasting psychological trauma. The use of napalm, along with other incendiary devices, brought about significant criticism and became a focal point for anti-war protests. Its impact extended beyond immediate destruction, as the intense burns and environmental damage it caused contributed to the suffering of civilians and combatants alike.

◻ ***DID YOU KNOW***

- The U.S. also dropped approximately 6.2 million tons of bombs on Vietnam, a staggering amount that was more than three times the tonnage dropped during World War II.

- The widespread bombing campaigns left an enduring impact, with 20% of Vietnam's total land area believed to still contain 800,000 tons of unexploded ordnance.

- Since the end of the war, over 100,000 casualties, including approximately 40,000 deaths, have occurred due to unexploded bombs and mines.

This deadly legacy of the Vietnam War continues to pose a severe threat to communities in Vietnam, hindering agricultural development and infrastructure expansion, and remains a painful reminder of the conflict's far-reaching consequences.

Laos, a neighboring country to Vietnam, holds the unfortunate distinction of being the most heavily bombed country per capita in history, largely due to the Vietnam War.

◘ DID YOU KNOW

- Over nine years, the United States dropped approximately 2 million tons of bombs on Laos, more than the total amount dropped on Germany and Japan combined during World War II.

Much of this bombing was part of the "Secret War" aimed at disrupting North Vietnamese supply lines, such as the Ho Chi Minh Trail. To this day, unexploded ordnance (UXO) poses a significant danger to the people of Laos, as undetonated bombs can still be found in fields, forests, and even residential areas, creating a constant threat to safety.

Bomber dropping bombs during Operation Linebacker

IX. Financial Cost: An Expensive Conflict

The Vietnam War came with an enormous financial cost.

- For the United States alone, the war cost approximately $168 billion, which would amount to roughly $1 trillion in today's terms.

This expenditure included everything from military operations and equipment to support for allied forces and post-war reparations. The financial burden of the war placed a strain on the U.S. economy, affecting government spending on domestic programs and contributing to inflation and economic challenges in the years following the conflict.

X. Protests: The Anti-War Movement and the Moratorium March

The Vietnam War was a turning point in American history not only for its combat but also for the scale of opposition it sparked on the home front.

☐ *DID YOU KNOW*

- One of the largest anti-war protests occurred on November 15, 1969, during the Moratorium March in Washington, D.C. Approximately 500,000 people participated, making it the largest anti-war rally in American history.

The protest was part of a wave of coordinated demonstrations that happened not just across the U.S., but around the world, with marches in places like London, Paris, and West Berlin. People were protesting for a lot of reasons - opposing the draft, anger over civilian casualties, and frustration with how the government was handling the war.

The anti-war movement had a huge impact on shaping public opinion and pushing U.S. policy as we'll see in a later chapter.

XI.☐The Technicality of "War" Status

Although commonly referred to as the "Vietnam War," this conflict was technically not a war by U.S. legal standards. According to the U.S. Constitution, Congress has the sole authority to declare war, and it has only done so six times, all during World War II. In the case of Vietnam, Congress authorized the deployment of troops but did not formally declare war. This distinction, while subtle, had significant implications for how the conflict was conducted and perceived, both domestically and internationally.

The lack of an official declaration of war allowed the U.S. government to engage in military operations without the same level of oversight that might accompany a formal war declaration. This ambiguity fueled debate over presidential powers and congressional oversight, leading to the passage of the War Powers Act in 1973, which sought to limit the president's ability to commit U.S. forces to foreign conflicts without congressional approval.

6. LIFE AS A SOLDIER

Ultimately, war is about people - the soldiers who endure difficult conditions, face unimaginable challenges, and navigate the physical and emotional tolls of conflict, with the Vietnam War being a prime example of how extreme and grueling those experiences could be. Let's take a look at who went to war and what they experienced.

I. Draft and Recruitment: The Mobilization of Young Soldiers

The Vietnam War is often seen as one of the most controversial chapters in American history, and a big reason for that was the draft. It brought countless young men into the military - many of them just teenagers or in their early twenties. Unlike earlier wars that relied more on volunteers, Vietnam leaned heavily on conscription, forcing many to serve whether they wanted to or not. This system stirred a lot of anger and resistance, especially since those drafted were often from lower-income families. It became a major flashpoint for anti-war protests, as young Americans were sent to fight in a distant, unfamiliar, and dangerous place far from home.

The United States draft system during the Vietnam War functioned through the Selective Service, a government agency responsible for identifying and inducting eligible men into military service. The draft targeted men aged 18 to 26, with exemptions for those in certain professions, enrolled in higher education, or suffering from medical conditions. Yet, the deferment options were often skewed towards young men from affluent backgrounds who could afford college or had connections to avoid the draft, while men from working-class or minority communities were more likely to be drafted.

As the war intensified, so did the demand for troops, leading to a tightening of deferments and the eventual drafting of men with lower academic or physical standards. For those eligible, the draft lottery was a defining and, at times, terrifying experience. Starting in December 1969, birthdays were drawn to determine the order of conscription, making a young man's date of birth a critical factor in whether he would be called up for duty. The draft lottery was broadcast nationwide, and the sight of friends and loved ones being called to service had a profound effect on families and communities.

The draft also prompted widespread resistance and anti-war activism. Many young men objected to being sent to Vietnam, a conflict they saw as politically motivated and morally ambiguous. Some sought deferments, while others found ways to avoid service altogether, sometimes fleeing to Canada or burning their draft cards in public protest.

The anti-draft movement fueled a larger anti-war sentiment across the country, sparking protests and demonstrations that brought national attention to the consequences of mandatory conscription. The draft ultimately became a deeply polarizing issue, influencing public opinion and increasing demands for an end to U.S. involvement in Vietnam.

Draft Resistance March, Yale University

Despite widespread opposition, thousands of young men were drafted and sent to Vietnam, facing the harsh realities of combat in a foreign land. Many were ill-prepared for the physical and emotional demands of warfare, having been hastily trained and thrust into a conflict unlike any other the United States had encountered.

II. The Jungle Environment, Combat, and Morale

The Jungle Terrain and Climate

For many American soldiers, the Vietnamese jungle was an overwhelming and often terrifying environment. The climate alone was a significant challenge: Vietnam's tropical weather brought intense heat, monsoon rains, and extreme humidity, making basic physical tasks exhausting and draining. The dense jungle vegetation, with its towering trees and thick underbrush, reduced visibility, creating a sense of isolation and constant vulnerability. Movement was slow and treacherous, as soldiers navigated through dense foliage and muddy terrain, often carrying heavy packs and equipment that weighed up to 50 pounds.

The terrain itself also contributed to the difficulty of combat. Vietnam's dense forests and rugged mountains provided ideal cover for the North Vietnamese Army (NVA) and Viet Cong guerrilla forces, who were skilled at using the landscape to their advantage. The Viet Cong set up a vast network of underground tunnels, enabling them to move undetected and launch surprise attacks. These tunnels also housed supply depots, hospitals, and command centers, providing a strategic advantage. American soldiers, unfamiliar with the jungle and its dangers, were often at a disadvantage against the guerrilla tactics of the Viet Cong, who could strike quickly and disappear before reinforcements arrived. The jungle environment created a constant sense of danger, as soldiers were never sure when or where the enemy might appear.

Soldiers had to contend with an array of tropical diseases and pests. Malaria, dysentery, and other illnesses were common, spread by insects and exacerbated by the unsanitary conditions of jungle warfare. Many soldiers also suffered from jungle rot, a painful skin infection caused by prolonged exposure to wet conditions. Leeches, venomous snakes, and insects were a constant nuisance, adding to the psychological strain of operating in such an environment. The combination of heat, humidity, and pests contributed to the soldiers' exhaustion and impacted their morale, as they struggled to adapt to an environment that felt both hostile and alien.

Combat Conditions and the Nature of Guerrilla Warfare

The combat conditions in Vietnam were markedly different from traditional warfare. The Americans faced an elusive enemy, well-versed in guerrilla tactics that relied on ambushes, booby traps, and hit-and-run attacks. The Viet Cong and NVA used the dense terrain to conceal their movements and set traps, such as punji sticks - sharp, bamboo stakes smeared with toxic substances - that could inflict severe injuries. Booby traps were an everyday hazard, with soldiers constantly on guard against hidden explosives, tripwires, and other traps. These tactics created a climate of fear and paranoia, as soldiers moved through the jungle with the knowledge that every step could be their last.

The nature of guerrilla warfare meant that there were few traditional battle lines. Instead, soldiers found themselves in a war without fronts, where danger could come from any direction and at any time. This unpredictability took a heavy toll on morale, as soldiers often felt they were fighting an invisible enemy. Even in villages, it was difficult to distinguish friend from foe, as Viet Cong fighters could blend in with the local population, leading to situations where American soldiers did not know whom to trust. This lack of clear objectives and the difficulty in identifying the enemy made the war feel both directionless and endless, undermining the sense of purpose that is essential for morale in combat.

Nighttime operations were particularly daunting. The Viet Cong often used the cover of darkness to launch surprise attacks, and American soldiers had to remain vigilant during the night, guarding their positions and preparing for possible assaults. The stress of constant vigilance led to sleep deprivation and fatigue, further affecting soldiers' physical and mental resilience. The darkness also heightened the isolation, sense of vulnerability and fear that many soldiers felt, as they faced an enemy adept at night fighting and familiar with the terrain.

▫ *DID YOU KNOW*

- U.S. Marine Chuck Mawhinney was the deadliest sniper in Vietnam. He recorded 103 confirmed kills and 216 probable kills in 16 months!

The Tunnel Rats

Let's take a look at one of the most dangerous jobs in the Vietnam War, that of the

Tunnel Rats!

Tunnel Rats were soldiers tasked with exploring and clearing the extensive network of underground tunnels built by the Viet Cong. These tunnels, often spanning hundreds of miles, were used for hiding, transporting supplies, storing weapons, and launching surprise attacks. Tunnel Rats were typically smaller soldiers, under 5ft 5 in or shorter, who could navigate the tight tunnels more easily.

U.S. soldiers had used CS gas blown into tunnel shafts to suffocate those inside. It also flooded area where they thought were tunnels, adding yellow dye to the water to enable aerial observers to spot tunnel entrances. Neither tactic was as successful as they hoped - many of the tunnels had several layers and doors built into for safety. This led to the U.S. sending down the Tunnel Rats!

Imagine what it would be like to enter a tunnel, armed with a flashlight, a pistol, and sometimes a knife, not knowing what you might find! Tunnel Rats entered the narrow, dark tunnels to locate booby traps, uncover enemy supplies, or find Viet Cong fighters hiding underground.

Entrance to Viet Cong tunnel

The tunnels were often filled with traps like punji sticks (sharpened bamboo spikes), trip wires, and explosives. Tunnel Rats had to carefully navigate and disarm these hazards. They often encountered Viet Cong fighters in the tunnels, where they fought in close-quarters combat.

The tunnels were incredibly tight and dark, making movement slow and visibility almost non-existent. In addition to coming across the enemy, they often faced snakes, rats, and other wildlife!

According to a former Viet Cong officer, the Tunnel Rats killed over 12,000 guerillas and captured many more. In a single operation in August 1968, the rats not only killed 3 Viet Cong but captured 153 more. Tunnel Rats uncovered most of the captured Viet Cong weapons and equipment.

The Tunnel Rats' role was crucial in disrupting Viet Cong operations, but it came with a heavy toll. Many suffered physical injuries or long-term psychological effects from their harrowing experiences. Their bravery and the vital nature of their work have since been recognized as a significant part of the Vietnam War's history.

☐ *DID YOU KNOW*

- 700 soldiers server as Tunnel Rats, with 36 killed, and 200 wounded, a casualty rate of 33%, high by even Vietnam War standards.

- The Viet Cong dug over 155 miles of tunnels. They were first dug in WW2 to fight the Japanese invasion.

- Initially hunting dogs were used to locate the enemy. The Viet Cong then began to use the same soap as the Americans, and in smelling the same as the Americans, the dogs were no longer able to locate the Vietnamese.

The Psychological Toll and Declining Morale

The harsh conditions of the jungle, combined with the unique and psychologically draining nature of guerrilla warfare, had a profound impact on the morale of American soldiers. The soldiers who fought in Vietnam were often younger and less experienced than those in previous wars, and the psychological toll of constant danger, isolation, and physical hardship left many struggling with mental health challenges. Many soldiers found it difficult to reconcile the harsh realities of combat with the unclear political objectives of the war, which contributed to feelings of disillusionment and frustration.

Morale among soldiers was further affected by the lack of public support for the war back home. Unlike the patriotic fervor that characterized previous conflicts, the Vietnam War was met with widespread opposition in the United States. Many soldiers were aware of the anti-war sentiment and felt disconnected from a society that often viewed them with suspicion or hostility. Letters from home sometimes reflected this division, and stories of protests, draft card burnings, and anti-war demonstrations left some soldiers feeling abandoned or even resented by the very people they were serving. This disconnect compounded the emotional burden they carried, leading to a sense of isolation not only from their surroundings in Vietnam but also from their own country.

Drug use became prevalent among troops as a way to cope with the physical and emotional strain of combat. Marijuana, opium, and heroin were relatively accessible in Vietnam, and some soldiers turned to these substances to numb the anxiety and stress, while others turned to alcohol. Substance abuse among soldiers became a concern for military commanders, who recognized that it was both a symptom of low morale and a factor that could further undermine discipline and effectiveness.

The experience of combat also led to what would later be recognized as post-traumatic stress disorder (PTSD). Many soldiers experienced symptoms of PTSD during their deployment, but the term and diagnosis were not formally recognized until years after the war as we will cover later.

Soldiers faced difficulties reintegrating into civilian life after returning from Vietnam, and were often met with indifference or hostility. The negative portrayal of the war in the media and the public's opposition to the conflict led to a lack of appreciation for the sacrifices made by those who served. Many veterans struggled to find meaning in their experiences, and the lack of support compounded their sense of isolation and disillusionment.

III. War Heroes

There was no shortage of heroes in the Vietnam War, with individuals displaying extraordinary courage and selflessness. Their actions exemplify the bravery and sacrifices made by countless soldiers during the conflict. 235 Medals of Honor were awarded during and immediately after the Vietnam War, with an additional 33 awards presented since 1978. Let's meet some of those heroes.

First Sergeant David H. McNerney

On March 22, 1967, McNerney and his unit were conducting a search and destroy mission near Polei Doc in South Vietnam when they were suddenly ambushed by a large North Vietnamese Army (NVA) force.

When his unit's commander was killed early in the attack, McNerney assumed command and personally led the fight against the overwhelming enemy force.

McNerney crawled through enemy fire to destroy a machine gun position with hand grenades, neutralizing a significant threat to his unit. Realizing the dire situation, he climbed a tree under enemy fire to mark the location for airstrikes, ensuring his unit received critical support.

Despite being wounded, McNerney refused to be evacuated. He stayed on the battlefield, encouraging his men and directing their efforts to repel the enemy attack. His leadership and bravery inspired his men to hold their ground against a numerically superior force, ultimately forcing the NVA to retreat.

McNerney's actions that day saved countless lives and exemplified extraordinary leadership, bravery, and selflessness. He was awarded the Medal of Honor for his valor and continued to serve in the Army until his retirement in 1969.

Specialist Four Leslie H. Sabo Jr.

Sabo Jr. was a U.S. Army soldier and posthumous recipient of the Medal of Honor for his extraordinary bravery during the Vietnam War.

On May 10, 1970, Sabo's unit, part of the 101st Airborne Division, was ambushed by a large enemy force in Se San, Cambodia. Despite being outnumbered and under heavy fire, Sabo displayed incredible courage and selflessness to protect his comrades.

Sabo immediately ran through a hail of gunfire to attack the enemy, killing several of them and disrupting their assault. This quick action allowed his unit to regroup and establish a defensive position.

While aiding a wounded comrade, Sabo used his own body as a shield to protect the soldier from further harm, displaying extraordinary selflessness.

Sabo also charged an enemy bunker that was pouring fire onto his unit. Despite being wounded by gunfire and a grenade, he managed to throw a grenade into the bunker, eliminating the threat.

Mortally wounded, Sabo continued to fight and distribute ammunition to his fellow soldiers. His final act of heroism was throwing himself on an enemy grenade to shield his comrades, sacrificing his life to save theirs.

Sabo's heroism went unrecognized for decades due to lost paperwork. It wasn't until

2012 that he was posthumously awarded the Medal of Honor by President Barack Obama.

Private Richard Norden

Norden was a 19-year-old Australian soldier who, in 1968, ran into enemy fire to help wounded soldiers during the Battle of Fire Support Base Coral. He carried a wounded section commander to safety, then returned to retrieve the body of another soldier. He was wounded himself, but went back a third time to clear the area and recover the body. His actions secured the enemy position and likely saved the lives of other soldiers.

He survived the war, but was only given the Victoria Cross, Australia's highest military award, after his death!

Captain Lance P. Sijan

In 1967, Sijan ejected from his aircraft over North Vietnam and evaded capture in the jungle for 46 days. During this time, he was seriously injured and suffered from shock and extreme weight loss due to lack of food.

After capture by North Vietnamese soldiers, he was tortured and beaten, but did not give the enemy any information. Due to his extreme weakness, adverse living conditions, insufficient clothing, and an inadequate diet, Captain Sijan contracted pneumonia and died in Hoa Lo prison camp. He was posthumously awarded the Medal of Honor in 1976.

Master Sergeant Roy Benavidez

Benavidez was known as the "unkillable Vietnam War Hero". In his first tour of duty, he stepped on a land mine, and doctors feared he would never walk again. After a year in hospital, he walked out of hospital, determined to return to Vietnam.

On May 2nd, 1968, a 12-man Special Forces patrol was surrounded by 1,000 NVA soldiers. Benavidez responded to an appeal for help, boarded a helicopter, and armed only with a knife, jumped from the helicopter when 30 feet from the ground, and went on the save the lives of 8 men.

During the six hours of continuous operations, Benavidez suffered severe wounds including: Seven major gunshot wounds, 28 shrapnel holes in his head, shoulder, buttocks, feet and legs, both arms slashed by a bayonet, right lung destroyed, and injuries to his mouth and the back of his head from being clubbed by a rifle butt. He was also shot in the back with an AK-47 and the bullet exited just beneath his heart!

When the battle was over and everyone evacuated, Benavidez was thought to be dead. As the doctor was about to zip up the body bag, Benavidez was able to spit, proving that somehow, after all he wounds, he was still alive!

In 1981, Benavidez received the Medal of Honor from President Reagan.

7. THE WAR BACK HOME

I. The Growing Anti-War Movement: Origins and Protests

The Vietnam War sparked a massive anti-war movement that would come to define the 1960s and 1970s in the United States. What began as a relatively small group of protesters soon blossomed into a widespread, national movement that attracted people from various walks of life, including students, veterans, intellectuals, and civil rights activists.

The movement's goals were to protest against the war itself, demand the withdrawal of American troops from Vietnam, and criticize the government's handling of the conflict.

Let's take a look at the origins of the anti-war movement, its major protests, and the key figures and groups involved in this essential part of American history.

The Origins of the Anti-War Movement

The roots of the anti-war movement can be traced back to the early years of U.S. involvement in Vietnam, which started with the Eisenhower administration's support for French colonialism in Indochina during the 1950s. As the United States progressively became more involved in the conflict, it was evident that the war would not be quick or easy. As reports of heavy U.S. casualties and the inability to effectively defeat the Viet Cong and North Vietnamese Army came to light, dissatisfaction with the war grew.

However, it wasn't until the early 1960s that a visible and vocal anti-war movement began to take shape. Initially, the movement was small and isolated, limited to a few left-wing intellectuals and activists who were already critical of the United States' foreign policy. One of the earliest significant moments in the development of the anti-war movement came in 1964, with the passage of the Gulf of Tonkin Resolution, which effectively gave Johnson the authority to use military force without a declaration of war. The American public, already uneasy about the conflict, began to see the escalation as a mistake.

Major Protests and Escalation of the Movement

In 1965, as the war dragged on, the anti-war movement began to gain momentum. The first large-scale protests took place on college campuses, particularly at universities like the University of California, Berkeley, and Columbia University in New York. Students protested against the war, viewing it as an unjust intervention in a foreign country that was unrelated to the United States' national security interests.

Protest at The Pentagon, October 1967

One of the most significant moments came on October 21st, 1967 when around 100,000 people gathered in a massive protest on the National Mall in Washington,

D.C. The event marked the first major anti-war demonstration that gained national attention. Protesters carried signs calling for the withdrawal of U.S. troops and the end of the war, and the rally helped galvanize opposition to the war throughout the country. The demonstration was also notable for its inclusion of a wide range of groups, from civil rights activists and labor unions to students and intellectuals.

In 1969, the anti-war movement reached new heights with the moratorium against the war, which took place on October 15th, 1969. It was the largest anti-war protest in U.S. history up to that point, with an estimated 2 million people participating in protests across the country. The movement also gained significant international support, as anti-Vietnam War demonstrations were held around the world, further isolating the United States on the global stage.

A major turning point in the movement occurred on May 4th, 1970, when Ohio National Guardsmen opened fire on students at Kent State University, killing four and wounding nine others. The incident shocked the nation and led to an explosion of protests on college campuses and in cities across the country. The deaths at Kent State served as a rallying cry for the anti-war movement, and the event remains one of the most tragic and influential moments in the history of the protests.

The growing number of protests, combined with the intense media coverage of the war, began to turn public opinion against the conflict. While the government continued to insist on the necessity of the war, the American people began to question the government's version of events, especially as the casualty count increased and the promises of success seemed increasingly distant.

The anti-war movement succeeded in pushing the issue to the forefront of American politics and helped bring about a change in public perception that eventually led to the U.S. withdrawal from Vietnam.

II.▫Who was Involved in the Anti-War Movement

The anti-war movement was not limited to college students or left-wing radicals; it was composed of a diverse range of people, including veterans, public figures, and civil rights activists. These individuals and groups played a crucial role in organizing protests, spreading the message of peace, and challenging the government's handling of the war.

Students and Campus Activism

One of the driving forces behind the anti-war movement was the student population. Many students, particularly at major universities, were deeply disillusioned by the government's actions in Vietnam. Groups such as Students for a Democratic Society (SDS) and the National Mobilization Committee to End the War in Vietnam (Mobe) were instrumental in organizing large-scale protests and sit-ins at campuses across the country.

Its efforts were focused not only on ending the war but also on pushing for greater political and social reforms in the United States. SDS became emblematic of the larger youth-driven counterculture movement, which sought to challenge traditional American values and institutions.

Protesters in Wichita, Kansas

Veterans Against the War

Perhaps one of the most powerful voices in the anti-war movement came from the veterans themselves. Veterans Against the Vietnam War (VVAW) was formed in 1967 by a group of former soldiers who had served in Vietnam. These veterans used their firsthand experiences to challenge the official narrative of the war and advocate for peace. The VVAW's efforts were especially impactful because they highlighted the personal costs of the war and the emotional and physical trauma that soldiers suffered.

One of the most poignant moments for the VVAW came in 1971 and the "Winter Soldier Investigation" in Detroit. Veterans testified about the war crimes and atrocities they had witnessed and committed in Vietnam. The testimony of these veterans was powerful and compelling, giving a human face to the anti-war movement and providing undeniable evidence of the brutality of the conflict.

Public Figures and Intellectuals

The anti-war movement also received significant support from public figures and intellectuals. Martin Luther King Jr., became a vocal critic of the war after 1967, when he publicly condemned the conflict in a speech at Riverside Church in New York. He argued that the war was immoral and a waste of American resources, detracting from efforts to address racial inequality and poverty in the United States. His stance on the war alienated many in the civil rights movement, but it also helped to build a broader anti-war coalition.

Norman Mailer, the author, was a vocal critic of the government's involvement in Vietnam, and his writing helped to shape public opinion about the conflict.

Jane Fonda, the actress, though initially criticized for her outspoken anti-war stance, became one of the most well-known public figures in the movement. She visited North Vietnam in 1972, where she was photographed sitting on an anti-aircraft gun, a moment that sparked outrage but also intensified the anti-war message.

The anti-war movement remains a significant chapter in American history, demonstrating the power of grassroots activism and the ability of ordinary citizens to affect change on a national level.

III. Media Coverage: Bringing the War Into American Living Rooms

The media had a large influence, particularly television news. The war in Vietnam was different from previous conflicts because it was the first "television war." The images of American soldiers fighting in the jungles of Vietnam, wounded and dying on the battlefield, and the carnage of bombed villages were broadcast on nightly news programs, often in vivid detail. This brought the brutal realities of war into American living rooms, making it harder for Americans to ignore the conflict or to believe the government's optimistic reports about progress in Vietnam.

The Terror of War, an iconic image of the Vietnam War, of children fleeing an accidental napalm attack

▫ *DID YOU KNOW*

- Photographer Nick Ut won a Pulitzer Prize for his 1972 image 'Terror of War". It centers on a nine-year-old girl called Kim Phúc, who was badly burned by the American napalm attack. Ut took Phúc and the other injured children to hospital, where it was thought her burns were so severe that she probably would not survive. After a 14-month hospital stay and 17 surgical procedures, including skin transplantations, she was able to return home. Now living in Canada, Phúc is a UNESCO Goodwill Ambassador and has launched a foundation to provide aid to child victims of war.

The media regularly featured updates on the war, including graphic images of combat and casualties, including the famous photograph of the execution of a Viet Cong suspect by a South Vietnamese officer. These images were powerful and unsettling, and they contrasted sharply with the rosy portrayals of the war provided by government officials. By 1969, a majority of Americans had turned against the war, and television news was a significant factor in that shift.

Viet Cong Prisoner awaits interrogation

Television journalists like Walter Cronkite played a particularly important role in shaping public opinion. Cronkite, the anchor of CBS Evening News, had established a reputation as a trusted figure in American journalism. After the Tet Offensive, he made a dramatic public statement in which he expressed his belief that the war was unwinnable, saying, "To say that we are mired in stalemate seems the only realistic if unsatisfactory conclusion." His skepticism about the war further helped sway the opinions of millions of Americans.

Television also broadcast scenes of the protests that were taking place across the United States. Images of demonstrators marching in the streets, students confronting

National Guardsmen, and anti-war leaders speaking out against the war became a familiar part of the media landscape. These images humanized the anti-war movement, showing that opposition to the war was not limited to radical activists, but was widespread and growing.

The combination of growing protests and graphic media coverage ultimately played a major role in influencing public opinion and pushing the government toward a revaluation of its policies in Vietnam.

8. THE SOCIAL CHANGES IN AMERICA

The Vietnam War unfolded against the backdrop of tremendous social and political upheaval in the United States, marked especially by the Civil Rights Movement and the rise of youth counterculture. These movements were interwoven in profound ways, as activists began to see connections between the fight for civil rights domestically and opposition to a war that disproportionately affected minority communities and the young. Civil rights leaders, particularly those representing African American communities, took strong stances against the war, emphasizing the racial injustices inherent in U.S. military involvement abroad and at home. Simultaneously, the war fueled a powerful youth counterculture, which questioned authority, challenged traditional gender roles, and promoted new, inclusive visions of patriotism.

I. Civil Rights and the Vietnam War

The Civil Rights Movement had been gaining momentum since the early 1950s, with African American activists calling for the end of segregation, disenfranchisement, and discrimination in the United States. By the time U.S. involvement in Vietnam began to escalate in the 1960s, the Civil Rights Movement was well underway, led by figures like Martin Luther King Jr., Malcolm X, and groups like the Southern Christian Leadership Conference (SCLC), the Congress of Racial Equality (CORE), and the Student Nonviolent Coordinating Committee (SNCC). While civil rights activism primarily focused on achieving racial equality and justice within the United States, many activists saw a strong connection between the war in Vietnam and the racial and economic injustices they were fighting at home.

The Role of African American Leaders in Opposing the War

African American leaders were among the earliest voices to publicly criticize U.S. involvement in Vietnam. One of the most significant figures in linking the Civil Rights Movement to anti-war activism was Dr. Martin Luther King Jr., who initially focused solely on domestic issues but gradually became one of the most prominent critics of the Vietnam War.

In his 1967 speech titled "Beyond Vietnam: A Time to Break Silence," King argued that the war was morally wrong and a direct betrayal of the United States' professed values of freedom and democracy. He contended that the war diverted resources away from domestic issues, particularly the fight against poverty, disproportionately affecting African American communities. King famously stated that the U.S. government was "the greatest purveyor of violence in the world today," a controversial stance that alienated him from some political allies but resonated with many African Americans and anti-war activists who saw the war as an extension of systemic racial oppression.

Malcolm X, although assassinated in 1965 before the height of anti-war protests, also emphasized the hypocrisy of a government that oppressed African Americans domestically while claiming to fight for freedom abroad. The sentiment Malcolm expressed laid the foundation for many black activists' opposition to the war, even after his death. Many African Americans saw the war as a distraction from the urgent needs of racial and economic justice at home, with black soldiers being sent to fight an enemy abroad while still being treated as second-class citizens in their own country.

African American Soldiers and Disproportionate Representation

The draft played a significant role in deepening opposition to the war within African American communities. African Americans were disproportionately drafted into combat roles in Vietnam due to a range of socio-economic factors, including systemic inequalities in education and employment, which limited their deferment options. Black soldiers faced significant discrimination within the military, often being assigned to the most dangerous positions. In 1965, African Americans made up around 11% of the U.S. population but constituted over 20% of the combat troops in Vietnam. This overrepresentation underscored the racial disparities that activists had long highlighted.

For African American soldiers, the irony of fighting for "freedom" abroad while still facing discrimination at home became painfully clear. The contradictions fueled resentment and politicization among many black soldiers, who returned home more committed to the fight for civil rights. Organizations like the Black Panthers linked the anti-war effort with the Civil Rights Movement, asserting that the Vietnam War was another form of oppression imposed on the poor and communities of color. The movement thus extended beyond the streets of America to the jungles of Vietnam, where black soldiers found solidarity in their shared experiences of injustice.

II. Youth and the Counterculture Movement

As opposition to the war spread, a powerful youth counterculture emerged, profoundly shaping American society. The Vietnam War became a focal point for young Americans, many of whom opposed the draft and the military-industrial complex that fueled the conflict. College campuses became hotbeds of anti-war activity, with students organizing protests, sit-ins, and teach-ins. The counterculture challenged traditional social norms, with young people questioning authority, redefining gender roles, and advocating for a vision of patriotism that opposed violence and imperialism.

The Draft and Youth Opposition to the War

The draft was one of the most contentious issues for young Americans. Until 1969, the Selective Service system was structured in a way that allowed deferments for college students, meaning that middle- and upper-class white men could often avoid combat duty. Working-class young men and young men of color, who had fewer educational opportunities, were disproportionately drafted into combat roles. For many young people, the draft highlighted the class and racial inequalities in American society, leading to increased opposition to the war.

The concept of "draft resistance" gained traction as young men refused to register, burned their draft cards, or fled to Canada. The Selective Service Act was revised in 1969 to create a lottery system, but by this time, resistance to the draft was widespread. The anti-draft movement became a powerful symbol of youth opposition to authority and the willingness of young Americans to risk legal repercussions in standing up against what they viewed as an unjust war.

Challenging Social Norms: Authority, Gender Roles, and Patriotism

The Vietnam War played a pivotal role in transforming American youth culture. The counterculture rejected traditional norms around authority, gender roles, and patriotism, forging a new social identity rooted in peace, equality, and personal freedom. Anti-war protests often went hand-in-hand with broader social movements, such as women's rights, gay rights, and environmentalism.

The counterculture movement challenged authority figures, including political leaders, the military, and law enforcement, who were seen as perpetuating a system of oppression and injustice. Young people questioned the validity of the "American Dream" as they saw their peers drafted and sent to fight in a war that many considered immoral. The phrase "Make love, not war" became a rallying cry, symbolizing the youth movement's rejection of traditional militaristic values.

Gender roles were also reevaluated as women joined the anti-war and civil rights movements in increasing numbers. The feminist movement intersected with the anti-war movement, as many women activists highlighted the links between militarism and patriarchy. The draft also sparked discussions about masculinity, as young men grappled with societal expectations of bravery and patriotism versus their personal beliefs and opposition to the war. Women and men together questioned the traditional roles assigned to them, advocating for a society based on equality and mutual respect.

A New Vision of Patriotism

For young Americans involved in the counterculture, the Vietnam War prompted a redefinition of patriotism. Rather than expressing love of country through unquestioning loyalty to the government, many young people began to see dissent as a patriotic duty. This new form of patriotism emphasized accountability and social justice, with activists arguing that the U.S. could only live up to its ideals of freedom and equality by addressing its flaws, both domestically and internationally.

The movement embraced alternative lifestyles that rejected consumerism, militarism, and social conformity. The "hippie" movement, as it came to be known, symbolized this rejection through its embrace of communal living, environmentalism, and peace activism. The war not only fueled anti-war sentiment but also encouraged young people to question the very structures of American society that allowed such a conflict to unfold.

Intersection of Civil Rights and Counterculture

The Civil Rights Movement and the counterculture of the 1960s intersected in their shared opposition to the Vietnam War and their broader critique of American society. Both movements saw the war as an extension of the same oppressive forces they were fighting against: racism, economic inequality, and unchecked authority. Figures like

Muhammad Ali, who famously refused to serve in Vietnam on religious and moral grounds, embodied this intersection. Ali's stance was particularly impactful because he highlighted the racial injustices African Americans faced, saying, "No Viet Cong ever called me [a racial slur]."

The anti-war and civil rights movements also shared a commitment to nonviolent protest and civil disobedience, drawing inspiration from earlier leaders like Mahatma Gandhi. As activists in both movements grew frustrated with the lack of progress, some turned to more militant approaches, exemplified by groups like the Black Panthers and the Weathermen. This shift reflected a growing impatience with the government's unwillingness to address systemic issues and a willingness to confront it directly.

III. Impact on Veterans

The Vietnam War left a profound and lasting impact on the soldiers who fought in it. Unlike veterans of previous wars, many returning from Vietnam faced unprecedented social, psychological, and physical challenges. Often stigmatized and even rejected by society, they returned to a country deeply divided over the war, and they struggled with complex mental health issues, including Post-Traumatic Stress Disorder (PTSD). Physical disabilities, both visible and hidden, also added to the hardships, as did the lack of adequate support systems for rehabilitation and reintegration.

Anti-War Sentiment - Social Rejection and Stigmatization

Vietnam War veterans returned home to a society that was markedly different from the one their predecessors had come back to after World War II or the Korean War. Unlike previous generations of veterans who were celebrated and honored for their service, Vietnam veterans were often met with indifference, ambivalence, or outright hostility.

With extensive television reporting, public outrage over events like the My Lai Massacre and the pervasive use of Agent Orange intensified anti-war sentiment and protests. Some Americans began to view soldiers as agents of an imperialistic war rather than individuals following orders in service to their country. As a result, veterans often encountered protests and negative reactions upon returning, with many civilians unfairly holding them accountable for the war's atrocities and failures. Unlike the parades and celebrations that had marked the end of World War II, there was nothing for the Vietnam veterans.

Many veterans felt marginalized, and struggled to reconcile their experiences in Vietnam with the hostile reception they received back home. Feelings of betrayal and isolation permeated their transition into civilian life. Many veterans did not feel comfortable discussing their experiences, fearing judgment or misunderstanding. This contributed to a long-standing stigma around Vietnam veterans that added to their sense of alienation and impacted their ability to reintegrate into society fully.

The Nature of Combat in Vietnam

The Vietnam War presented unique psychological challenges, as soldiers faced guerrilla warfare tactics, an unclear enemy, and ambiguous frontlines. They were often subjected to surprise attacks, ambushes, and booby traps, which created a pervasive sense of danger even in seemingly safe areas. The concept of "search and destroy" missions put soldiers in constant exposure to life-threatening situations, and the lines between civilians and combatants were often blurred. Such conditions fostered a sense of hypervigilance and heightened stress, making it challenging to distinguish between safe and hostile environments.

▢ *DID YOU KNOW*

- It's estimated that booby traps caused around 11% of US causalities in the Vietnam War.

Many soldiers witnessed the deaths of friends and fellow soldiers, leading to what is known as "survivor's guilt." They often questioned why they had survived while others had not, which contributed to long-lasting feelings of guilt and depression. The psychological strain of these experiences was compounded by the inability of many veterans to find understanding or validation for their experiences upon returning to the United States.

The Emergence of PTSD as a Diagnosis

The term "Post-Traumatic Stress Disorder" (PTSD) wasn't officially recognized by the American Psychiatric Association until 1980, several years after the Vietnam War ended. However, its recognition as a distinct mental health condition was partially influenced by the experiences of Vietnam veterans who suffered from chronic psychological symptoms. Studies and testimonies revealed that many veterans were experiencing flashbacks, nightmares, intrusive thoughts, emotional numbness, irritability, and difficulty with emotional regulation. The PTSD diagnosis acknowledged that such symptoms were normal responses to the extreme stress of combat.

However, even with this newfound understanding, many veterans were reluctant to seek treatment due to the stigma associated with mental health issues. The lack of comprehensive support systems left many without adequate access to mental health care. This resulted in long-term consequences, including substance abuse, homelessness, and suicide, which became widespread issues within the Vietnam veteran community.

Agent Orange and Long-Term Health Effects

One of the most infamous legacies of the Vietnam War is the extensive use of herbicides, particularly Agent Orange, which was deployed to defoliate dense jungles and eliminate cover for enemy forces. Agent Orange contained dioxin, a toxic chemical known to cause severe health issues, including various cancers, neurological disorders, skin conditions, and birth defects. The U.S. Department of Veterans Affairs (VA) has since recognized that Agent Orange exposure is associated with diseases like Parkinson's, diabetes, and certain forms of cancer.

Veterans exposed to Agent Orange suffered from debilitating health problems that often went unacknowledged for years. Initially, the government denied any connection between Agent Orange exposure and these health issues, leaving veterans without the medical support or disability compensation they needed. After decades of advocacy and legal battles, the VA eventually began to offer compensation and medical care for Agent Orange-related conditions. However, for many veterans, this acknowledgment came too late, as they had already endured years of suffering.

Physical Injuries and Rehabilitation Challenges

Many Vietnam veterans returned home with serious physical injuries, including amputations, spinal injuries, and other disabilities resulting from gunfire, explosions, and accidents. Advances in medical care meant that more soldiers survived injuries that would have been fatal in previous conflicts, but they often returned with significant impairments that required long-term rehabilitation.

The U.S. military's medical and rehabilitation facilities were often ill-equipped to handle the high volume of wounded soldiers. Veterans faced lengthy wait times for treatment, limited access to specialized care, and bureaucratic obstacles when applying for disability benefits. Many veterans struggled to find employment due to physical disabilities, further compounding their difficulties in adjusting to civilian life. The lack of adequate support for physical rehabilitation not only affected veterans' physical well-being but also contributed to psychological challenges, as they struggled to regain a sense of purpose and normalcy.

Substance Abuse and Homelessness

The combination of psychological trauma, social isolation, and physical disabilities led many Vietnam veterans to turn to substance abuse as a coping mechanism. Alcohol and drug use became prevalent among veterans attempting to manage the symptoms of PTSD and the distress of reintegration into an unwelcoming society. In some cases, soldiers were exposed to drugs during their time in Vietnam, where substances like marijuana, heroin, and opium were readily available. Returning home, they continued to use these substances as a way to cope with their pain and trauma.

Substance abuse, in turn, exacerbated other issues, leading to job loss, family breakdown, and in many cases, homelessness. According to studies conducted in the 1980s and 1990s, Vietnam veterans accounted for a significant proportion of homeless individuals, with PTSD and substance abuse being major contributing factors.

Long-Term Societal and Policy Impacts

The challenges faced by Vietnam veterans catalyzed broader societal and policy changes regarding how the United States treats its military personnel and veterans. The inadequate support provided to Vietnam veterans led to the establishment of various programs and reforms aimed at improving veterans' health care, mental health services, and social reintegration support.

The Evolution of Veteran Care Programs

In response to public pressure and advocacy by veterans' groups, the Department of Veterans Affairs gradually expanded its services, particularly in the area of mental health care. The VA implemented counseling programs for PTSD and provided additional resources for veterans struggling with substance abuse and homelessness. The VA's "Vet Centers," which offer counseling for combat veterans, were established to help veterans readjust to civilian life.

Legislation like the Agent Orange Act of 1991 recognized the connection between chemical exposure and health issues, leading to expanded benefits for affected veterans, and a more comprehensive approach to veteran care, recognizing both the visible and invisible wounds of war.

Changing Attitudes Toward Mental Health and Military Service

The experiences of Vietnam veterans helped reshape societal attitudes toward mental health, especially concerning PTSD. Their struggles raised awareness about the psychological toll of combat, contributing to a broader cultural understanding of mental health issues. This shift in perception has influenced how the military and society approach mental health in subsequent conflicts, leading to earlier intervention, better support systems, and a more proactive approach to addressing PTSD and other combat-related mental health conditions.

9. THE END OF THE WAR AND ITS AFTERMATH

I. The U.S. Withdrawal and the Fall of Saigon: The Costs and Consequences of the Vietnam War

The Vietnam War came to a turbulent end with the U.S. withdrawal and the fall of Saigon in 1975. The conflict, which spanned nearly two decades, drew to a close after prolonged peace talks, intense battles, and a significant toll on the soldiers and civilians involved.

The legacy of the war, however, endures, marked by its human, economic, and political costs. For both the United States and Southeast Asia, the costs were significant, shaping regional dynamics and altering the lives of millions. Understanding the complex process of the U.S. withdrawal, the political shifts that occurred during peace talks, and the eventual fall of Saigon provides insight into the far-reaching consequences of the war on Vietnam, Southeast Asia, and the United States itself.

The U.S. Withdrawal and the Fall of Saigon: A Gradual Retreat

Peace Talks and the Path to Withdrawal

After years of intense and costly fighting, peace talks aimed at ending the Vietnam War began in Paris in 1968. These negotiations brought together representatives from North Vietnam, South Vietnam, the United States, and the Viet Cong. However, progress was slow and marred by frequent breakdowns as both sides clung to vastly different goals and terms. For North Vietnam and the Viet Cong, a unified Vietnam under communist control was non-negotiable. In contrast, the United States and South Vietnam sought to maintain a non-communist government in the South, preserving what they saw as a bulwark against communist expansion in Southeast Asia.

Despite these efforts, peace talks stalled repeatedly due to disagreements over prisoner releases, the future of the South Vietnamese government, and the fate of U.S.-backed President Nguyen Van Thieu.

As negotiations dragged on, Nixon authorized extensive bombing campaigns in

North Vietnam and Laos, known as the "Christmas Bombing" in December 1972, to pressure North Vietnamese leaders into accepting a ceasefire. Ultimately, on January 27th, 1973, the Paris Peace Accords were signed. This agreement led to a formal ceasefire, allowed for the return of American POWs, and stipulated that the United States would withdraw the remainder of its troops from Vietnam within 60 days.

The ceasefire quickly broke down, and both North and South Vietnam resumed fighting almost immediately. Without American support, the South Vietnamese government struggled to hold back the North Vietnamese forces. Despite billions in U.S. military aid, South Vietnam was increasingly isolated as the U.S. public and Congress were unwilling to provide further direct military intervention. By early 1975, North Vietnamese forces were advancing toward Saigon, capturing one city after another in a rapid offensive.

The Fall of Saigon

The final chapter of the Vietnam War unfolded in the spring of 1975, as North Vietnamese forces launched their decisive assault on Saigon. The fall of Saigon was swift and chaotic. By April, it became clear that South Vietnam could no longer hold back the advancing North Vietnamese Army (NVA). American officials scrambled to evacuate remaining U.S. personnel and at-risk South Vietnamese citizens as communist forces closed in on the city. On April 29th, 1975, the U.S. launched Operation Frequent Wind, the largest helicopter evacuation in history, airlifting thousands of American personnel and Vietnamese refugees from Saigon to U.S. ships offshore. These scenes, marked by frantic crowds gathering at the U.S. Embassy and desperate South Vietnamese citizens clinging to helicopters, would become emblematic of the war's tragic end.

On April 30th, 1975, North Vietnamese tanks rolled into Saigon, marking the official end of the war. The city fell with little resistance, and the South Vietnamese government surrendered unconditionally. The fall of Saigon marked a victory for North Vietnam and the reunification of the country under communist rule. It was a symbolic and humiliating end for the United States, which had invested so much in supporting the South Vietnamese government only to see it collapse. For many Americans, the images of the evacuation and the fall of Saigon symbolized the war's tragic and costly nature, sparking debates about American interventionism and foreign policy.

II. The Costs of War

Human Costs

The Vietnam War inflicted severe human costs on both Americans and the Vietnamese population. For the United States, over 58,000 American soldiers were killed, and more than 150,000 were wounded. Many veterans returned home physically and psychologically scarred, facing challenges such as post-traumatic stress disorder (PTSD). The war deeply affected the families of soldiers and created divisions within American society as the anti-war movement grew, challenging the morality and necessity of the U.S. involvement in Vietnam.

The war's toll on Vietnam was even more devastating. Estimates suggest that nearly 2 million Vietnamese civilians died, along with approximately 1 million North Vietnamese and Viet Cong soldiers and over 200,000 South Vietnamese soldiers. Civilian casualties were particularly high due to intense bombing campaigns, chemical warfare, and guerilla combat that blurred the lines between combatants and civilians.

The U.S. military dropped an estimated 6.2 million tons of bombs on Vietnam, more than triple the amount used during World War II. Many rural areas were left ravaged by defoliants like Agent Orange, which caused long-term health issues, including cancers, birth defects, and other serious health problems that continue to affect Vietnamese families today.

Economic Costs

The financial burden of the Vietnam War on the United States was immense. The conflict cost the U.S. approximately $168 billion, equivalent to about $1 trillion in today's terms. This expenditure included military operations, equipment, and support for allied forces, as well as care for veterans and other post-war obligations. The cost of the war placed a heavy strain on the American economy, contributing to inflation and diverting funds from domestic programs. This reallocation of resources led to reduced investment in infrastructure, education, and social programs, impacting American society long after the war had ended.

For Vietnam, the economic damage was catastrophic. The relentless bombing campaigns and widespread use of chemical defoliants destroyed large swathes of arable land, decimated forests, and poisoned rivers and streams. The war's economic impact was further compounded by the loss of life and displacement of millions, which left the country without the manpower necessary for rebuilding. Even after reunification, Vietnam faced enormous challenges in rebuilding its economy and infrastructure. International isolation and limited foreign aid from its communist allies meant that recovery was slow and challenging.

Political Costs

Politically, the Vietnam War had profound implications for both the United States and Southeast Asia. In the U.S., the war deepened societal divisions and led to widespread distrust in government. The Pentagon Papers revealed that successive U.S. administrations had misled the public about the scope and progress of the war, weakening Americans' faith in their leaders. The war also sparked changes in U.S. foreign policy, as Congress passed the War Powers Act in 1973 to limit the president's ability to engage in military conflicts without congressional approval.

In Southeast Asia, the fall of Saigon and the victory of communist forces in Vietnam had a domino effect, as neighboring countries such as Cambodia and Laos also experienced communist takeovers. In Cambodia, the Khmer Rouge, led by Pol Pot, took control in 1975 and launched a brutal regime that resulted in the deaths of an estimated 2 million people through forced labor, starvation, and genocide. The destabilization of the region left deep scars and led to humanitarian crises and waves of refugees seeking safety.

Vietnam itself, now under communist rule, faced the complex challenge of integrating the North and South, with stark differences in political beliefs, economies, and social structures. Although the country achieved reunification, it remained isolated from much of the international community, particularly the West, and had limited resources for post-war recovery.

III.□Vietnam After the War: Rebuilding and the Path to Economic Reform

The Vietnam War reshaped the country in every way. Reunification was only the beginning of a new set of challenges. Vietnam faced the immense task of rebuilding a country devastated by war, poverty, and isolation. In the decades that followed, the Vietnamese government sought to stabilize the nation, leading it through an arduous journey of economic reforms and opening the doors to global integration.

Today, Vietnam stands as a testament to resilience and transformation, but its path to recovery was fraught with difficulty. Examining the years after the war reveals Vietnam's struggles and its eventual economic transformation, which laid the foundation for the country's modern growth.

Rebuilding a War-Torn Nation: The Immediate Challenges

The Vietnam War had left the country in shambles. The infrastructure was in ruins, with cities like Hanoi and Saigon (renamed Ho Chi Minh City) extensively damaged from years of bombing and fighting. The rural landscape was also deeply affected, as large areas of arable land had been scorched, defoliated, or contaminated by chemical agents like Agent Orange, which had long-term health effects on the population. Alongside the physical devastation was an equally daunting social cost: millions of people had been killed, injured, or displaced, and the divide between the North and South persisted, even after the formal reunification.

Basic needs like housing, healthcare, and education were in critical demand, and there was a severe shortage of skilled labor. Much of the country's economic infrastructure had been destroyed, leaving Vietnam dependent on a largely agrarian economy that was insufficient for sustained growth.

Recognizing the need to rebuild, the government pursued an ambitious reconstruction plan, attempting to quickly industrialize and modernize the economy. However, these efforts were hampered by the country's isolation from the Western world and limited support from its communist allies, the Soviet Union and China.

Post-War Policies: Collectivization and the Push for Communism

The Vietnamese government, under the leadership of the Communist Party, implemented socialist policies to consolidate its control and achieve economic independence. These policies included the collectivization of agriculture, nationalization of private industries, and the establishment of state-owned enterprises. Modeled on the policies of China and the Soviet Union, these measures aimed to create a centrally planned economy that would eliminate capitalist influences and ensure equal distribution of resources among citizens.

Collectivization, however, faced significant resistance, particularly in the South, where private ownership of land and businesses was more common and culturally ingrained. Farmers were required to work in collective farms where the government dictated production quotas, deciding which crops to grow and setting fixed prices. This approach aimed to boost agricultural productivity and redistribute wealth, but in practice, it led to a severe drop in production. Farmers had little incentive to produce more than their quotas, leading to food shortages, decreased output, and widespread poverty. The policy was unpopular, especially in the southern regions, where many had previously enjoyed relative prosperity under a market-oriented economy.

Industrial nationalization was similarly problematic. Factories and businesses were taken over by the state, but the government's lack of experience in managing large-scale industries resulted in inefficiency, corruption, and a stagnating economy. State-owned enterprises struggled to remain productive, and Vietnam found itself facing economic stagnation. By the early 1980s, the nation was on the brink of collapse, with widespread food shortages, soaring inflation, and low productivity crippling the economy.

Diplomatic Isolation and the Impact of Cold War Politics

Vietnam's diplomatic isolation compounded its economic woes. Following the end of the war, Vietnam had tense relations with China, despite their shared communist ideology. Border skirmishes erupted in 1979, leading to a short but intense conflict between Vietnam and China. The border war further strained Vietnam's resources and created a lingering sense of hostility that impacted regional trade and security.

Vietnam's involvement in Cambodia, where it intervened to topple the Khmer Rouge regime in 1978, led to further isolation from the global community. The United States and other Western nations viewed this intervention as an act of aggression and imposed economic sanctions, isolating Vietnam from the Western financial and trade networks. The Soviet Union provided some support, but it was insufficient to sustain

Vietnam's struggling economy, and by the 1980s, the country was in dire need of change.

Doi Moi: The Turning Point of Economic Reform

Faced with economic crisis and international isolation, Vietnamese leaders recognized the need for a drastic shift in policy. In 1986, the Communist Party introduced a series of economic reforms under the policy known as "Doi Moi," which translates to "Renovation." Doi Moi marked a decisive turn away from strict central planning toward a socialist-oriented market economy, aiming to combine the advantages of socialism with elements of a free-market system.

Under Doi Moi, the government allowed private ownership of businesses and land, encouraging individual entrepreneurship and foreign investment. Farmers were no longer required to work in collectives; instead, they were permitted to own land, make independent production decisions, and sell their crops at market prices. This increased agricultural productivity dramatically, making Vietnam one of the largest exporters of rice and coffee within a decade.

In the industrial sector, the government began privatizing state-owned enterprises, giving managers more autonomy and encouraging foreign direct investment (FDI). Vietnam enacted laws to attract foreign companies, offering incentives such as tax breaks and the protection of foreign assets. This shift in policy resulted in a flood of investment, particularly from Asian countries like Japan and South Korea, fueling rapid industrialization.

Vietnam's embrace of economic reform had a profound impact on its development. Between 1986 and 1996, the country's GDP grew significantly, poverty rates fell, and the quality of life improved as living standards rose across the country. Doi Moi also laid the foundation for a more open society, as economic growth brought about changes in education, healthcare, and urban infrastructure.

Economic Integration and Globalization

In the 1990s, Vietnam continued to reintegrate itself into the international community. Diplomatic relations with the United States were normalized in 1995, opening new trade opportunities and contributing to economic growth. That same year,

Vietnam joined the Association of Southeast Asian Nations (ASEAN), marking its return to the regional fold and strengthening its ties with neighboring countries.

Vietnam's entry into the World Trade Organization (WTO) in 2007 marked a significant milestone in its economic transformation. Membership in the WTO helped Vietnam gain access to global markets, diversify its economy, and increase exports. As Vietnam embraced international trade, foreign investments surged, especially in manufacturing and technology, turning the country into a hub for global supply chains. This led to the creation of millions of jobs and stimulated growth across multiple industries.

Social and Cultural Impacts of Economic Reforms

The economic reforms and increased engagement with the world led to significant changes in Vietnamese society. As the economy grew, urbanization accelerated, with major cities like Hanoi and Ho Chi Minh City transforming into bustling metropolises. Improvements in education and healthcare accompanied these shifts, and Vietnam began investing in its human capital, resulting in a younger generation more exposed to global ideas and cultures.

Economic reform also brought about changes in the social structure of the country. A new middle class emerged, benefitting from better job opportunities, higher incomes, and improved living standards. Consumerism rose as people had access to a broader array of goods and services, including modern technology and Western products. The influence of the internet and social media, particularly among the youth, has played a role in shaping a more open and diverse culture, allowing for greater freedom of expression than in previous decades.

Environmental and Developmental Challenges

While economic reforms have lifted millions out of poverty and stimulated economic growth, Vietnam's rapid development has also brought challenges, particularly regarding environmental sustainability. Industrialization, urbanization, and increased agricultural production have led to pollution, deforestation, and depletion of natural resources. The Mekong Delta, a crucial region for rice production, is facing ecological stress due to both climate change and human activities, threatening food security in the region.

While Doi Moi has led to remarkable growth, regional disparities remain. Urban centers like Ho Chi Minh City and Hanoi have experienced rapid development, but many rural areas continue to lag behind, lacking infrastructure, healthcare, and educational opportunities. The government now faces the challenge of achieving balanced development that benefits both urban and rural populations, ensuring sustainable growth and reducing inequality.

10. THE LEGACY OF THE VIETNAM WAR

The Vietnam War marked a transformative period in American history, profoundly shaping public opinion, foreign policy, and cultural expression. Its effects extended far beyond the battlefield, leading to shifts in American foreign policy and inspiring significant representations in popular culture.

Let's take a look at the "Vietnam Syndrome," a term describing the cautious approach to military intervention that emerged in the United States following the Vietnam War.

I.□Vietnam Syndrome and Changes in U.S. Foreign Policy

The term "Vietnam Syndrome" describes the widespread American reluctance to engage in military intervention abroad following the prolonged and deeply controversial Vietnam War. This war was a national trauma, as it challenged Americans' faith in their government, questioned the ethics of interventionism, and raised skepticism about the U.S.'s role as a global "policeman." The war's devastating human and economic costs - 58,220 American lives lost, hundreds of thousands injured, millions of Vietnamese civilians and soldiers killed, and billions of dollars expended - left the American public and policymakers wary of entering future conflicts without clear objectives or exit strategies.

Emergence of Vietnam Syndrome

"Vietnam Syndrome" first emerged in the 1970s as policymakers and the American public alike grappled with the aftermath of the Vietnam War. Unlike World War II, which was largely perceived as a justified fight against global fascism, the Vietnam War lacked a clear moral imperative. The war's prolonged nature, coupled with widespread media coverage and graphic depictions of violence, led to growing domestic opposition.

This social opposition left a lasting impact on American politics. Policymakers became increasingly aware that public support was essential for any military endeavor. The war exposed the risks of entanglement in distant conflicts, particularly those rooted in complex local and ideological disputes. As a result, "Vietnam Syndrome" became shorthand for the collective American aversion to overseas military intervention, particularly in conflicts without direct threats to national security.

Vietnam Syndrome in Action: The Carter and Reagan Eras

In the years immediately following the Vietnam War, presidents faced significant pressure to avoid another costly conflict. President Jimmy Carter, elected in 1976, took office with a foreign policy approach that emphasized human rights, diplomacy, and reducing military interventions. Carter's administration sought to shift focus from Cold War rivalries to cooperative international relations. However, as the Soviet Union expanded its influence in areas like Afghanistan and as Iran fell into revolution, American concerns about maintaining global power resurged, challenging Carter's avoidance of military action.

The election of President Ronald Reagan in 1980 marked a shift toward a more assertive foreign policy. Reagan believed that overcoming "Vietnam Syndrome" required restoring American confidence in its military and foreign policy, yet he still faced the legacy of caution from the Vietnam experience. While Reagan promoted a strong military and supported anti-communist movements globally, he often opted for indirect involvement, using economic sanctions and CIA-backed operations instead of full-scale military intervention. Notably, Reagan's approach was exemplified in the use of proxy forces in Nicaragua and military advisors in El Salvador, efforts aimed at countering Soviet influence without large-scale troop deployments.

Reagan's response to "Vietnam Syndrome" also included a dramatic moment in 1983 when he deployed U.S. Marines to Lebanon as part of a peacekeeping force. However, after the 1983 Beirut barracks bombing that killed 241 U.S. service members, public support quickly dwindled, and Reagan eventually withdrew troops, underscoring the continued impact of Vietnam-era caution on American foreign policy decisions.

The Gulf War and the Temporary "End" of Vietnam Syndrome

By the late 1980s, many policymakers and military leaders believed that "Vietnam Syndrome" was restraining the U.S.'s ability to respond effectively to international crises. President George H.W. Bush's administration aimed to overcome this reluctance by rallying public and international support for the Gulf War in 1991. Unlike

Vietnam, the Gulf War had a clear objective - liberate Kuwait from Iraqi occupation - and enjoyed substantial international backing, including support from the United Nations.

Bush's handling of the Gulf War seemed to dispel "Vietnam Syndrome" temporarily. The swift, decisive victory restored confidence in the U.S. military's capabilities and led to a wave of patriotic fervor. However, "Vietnam Syndrome" did not disappear entirely. The brief, successful Gulf War was perceived as an exception, not a new norm, and the cautious approach to intervention reemerged in the Obama era, particularly as the wars in Iraq and Afghanistan became prolonged and controversial conflicts reminiscent of Vietnam.

II.◻Vietnam in Popular Culture

The Vietnam War significantly influenced American popular culture, inspiring a wide array of films, music, literature, and art. These works captured the complex emotions surrounding the war, from anger and disillusionment to grief and reflection. The cultural output related to Vietnam often highlighted the war's moral ambiguity, the psychological toll on soldiers, and the division within American society.

Films and the Cinematic Representation of Vietnam

Films about Vietnam range from realistic portrayals of combat to psychological dramas exploring the moral and emotional impacts of war. Some of the most famous Vietnam War movies emerged in the late 1970s and 1980s, including Apocalypse Now (1979), The Deer Hunter (1978), Platoon (1986), and Full Metal Jacket (1987). These films went beyond simple war narratives, instead focusing on the darkness of human nature, the chaos of the Vietnam conflict, and the soldiers' struggles with morality and mental health.

Apocalypse Now, directed by Francis Ford Coppola, was loosely based on Joseph Conrad's novella Heart of Darkness and depicted a journey into the moral void of the Vietnam War. With haunting scenes and surreal imagery, the film portrayed war as an all-consuming force that stripped soldiers of their humanity. The Deer Hunter, directed by Michael Cimino, explored the psychological impact of war on a small group of friends from a Pennsylvania steel town, focusing on their harrowing experiences in Vietnam and the trauma they faced upon returning home.

Platoon, directed by Oliver Stone, who was himself a Vietnam veteran, offered a more direct critique of the war. It highlighted the brutal realities of combat and the division among soldiers, providing an unfiltered look at the violence and moral ambiguity of the war. These films, though fictional, created an enduring image of Vietnam as a nightmarish and morally confusing conflict, cementing the war's reputation as a psychological and societal wound.

Music and the Soundtrack of Dissent

Music played a central role in shaping public perception of the Vietnam War, with anti-war songs becoming a soundtrack to the protest movement. Iconic songs like Bob Dylan's "Blowin' in the Wind," Creedence Clearwater Revival's "Fortunate Son," and Edwin Starr's "War" voiced frustration with the war and its impact on American society.

Dylan's "Blowin' in the Wind" became an anthem for both the civil rights and anti-war movements, posing rhetorical questions about peace, justice, and freedom. Creedence Clearwater Revival's "Fortunate Son" expressed resentment toward the privileged elite who avoided military service, while working-class Americans were sent to fight. Edwin Starr's "War," with its emphatic refrain "War - what is it good for? Absolutely nothing," became an unmistakable protest anthem, denouncing the futility and destructiveness of the Vietnam War.

Musicians like Jimi Hendrix, Janis Joplin, and Joan Baez performed songs that resonated with the counterculture's anti-establishment values. Woodstock, the legendary 1969 music festival, symbolized the intersection of music, protest, and the countercultural opposition to the Vietnam War, solidifying music as an essential platform for anti-war sentiment.

Literature and the Personal Experience of War

Literature about the Vietnam War has provided a powerful means for veterans and authors to process and convey their experiences. Some of the most significant works include The Things They Carried by Tim O'Brien, Dispatches by Michael Herr, and Born on the Fourth of July by Ron Kovic. These books helped illuminate the personal toll of the war, blending memoir, fiction, and journalism to explore the complexities of military service and the psychological scars left by combat.

The Things They Carried, a semi-autobiographical novel by Tim O'Brien, is a collection of linked short stories that delve into the emotional burden carried by soldiers. Through narrative fragmentation, O'Brien captures the surreal and often contradictory experiences of soldiers, emphasizing the blend of fear, courage, and trauma that defined their time in Vietnam.

Michael Herr's Dispatches, based on his work as a war correspondent, offers a raw, unfiltered view of the combat zone, portraying the adrenaline-fueled experiences of soldiers and the absurdity of the war. Ron Kovic's Born on the Fourth of July, a memoir detailing his life as a disabled veteran and anti-war activist, exposed the neglect and marginalization faced by Vietnam veterans upon their return home, emphasizing the war's human cost.

III.◻How the Vietnam War Shaped Modern America

The Vietnam War influenced modern America in several ways, transforming its social and political landscape and challenging its national identity. For the first time in history, Americans were exposed to a brutal and controversial war on a daily basis through uncensored media coverage, intensifying anti-war sentiment and skepticism toward the government. This experience laid the foundation for modern American political discourse, fostering a more questioning attitude toward authority and creating a legacy of civic engagement that has influenced generations.

Increased Skepticism Toward Authority

Prior to Vietnam, Americans generally trusted their leaders and believed in the integrity of governmental decisions, particularly in foreign policy. However, as the war dragged on with no clear end in sight, confidence in the government eroded. The revelations of the Pentagon Papers in 1971 exposed systematic deception on the part of multiple presidential administrations, showing that officials had consistently misled the public about the war's progress and the likelihood of victory.

The American public became increasingly aware of the "credibility gap" between what government officials claimed and the reality on the ground in Vietnam. This realization spurred a new era of distrust in government, with Americans questioning the motives and transparency of their leaders. This skepticism carried into subsequent decades, affecting public opinion on issues ranging from Watergate to the Iraq War. The war instilled a vigilance that has continued to shape American civic culture, encouraging citizens to hold their leaders accountable and scrutinize the government's actions more closely than before.

Transformation of Political Engagement

The Vietnam War also reshaped the nature of political engagement in the United States. The anti-war movement mobilized millions of Americans, and created an unprecedented level of political involvement, spurring citizens who had previously been apolitical or disengaged to participate in the democratic process. Activism during the Vietnam era created a framework for organizing and mobilizing that would later inspire other social movements, including the civil rights, women's rights, and environmental movements.

The activism during this period emphasized grassroots organizing, with ordinary citizens forming networks and groups to advocate for change. Students played a pivotal role in organizing large-scale anti-war protests and fostering political awareness on college campuses. This political energy spilled over into the voting booth, as younger Americans, emboldened by their anti-war activism, became more invested in elections and legislative change.

The passage of the 26th Amendment in 1971, which lowered the voting age from 21 to 18, was a direct response to the Vietnam War. Young Americans argued that if they were old enough to be drafted and fight in a foreign war, they should also be able to vote. It empowered young voters, and also demonstrated the tangible impact of collective political action, reinforcing a generation's belief in their ability to shape national policy.

Shifts in Social Norms and Cultural Attitudes

Beyond political engagement, the Vietnam War had a significant cultural impact. As anti-war sentiments grew, they fueled the counterculture movement, which rejected traditional values and questioned established social norms. This period saw a rise in questioning authority figures, from the government to the military, and even traditional family structures. The youth of the 1960s and 1970s, affected by the disillusionment of Vietnam, began advocating for more egalitarian and progressive values, which led to changes in gender roles, relationships, and expectations.

The skepticism and disillusionment born of the Vietnam era influenced American cultural expressions in film, music, and art, creating an enduring shift in how Americans understood patriotism and loyalty. For many, true patriotism became associated not with unquestioning allegiance to authority but with standing up for justice, peace, and integrity. This shift toward a more critical and self-reflective patriotism became a hallmark of post-Vietnam American identity.

IV. Remembering Vietnam: Memorials, Recognition, and Enduring Lessons

The importance of remembering the Vietnam War and honoring those who served cannot be overstated. The memory of Vietnam is preserved not only through history books and media but also through memorials, public ceremonies, and ongoing recognition of the sacrifices made by veterans. These acts of remembrance are essential to acknowledging the cost of war and the personal toll it takes on soldiers, their families, and society as a whole.

The Vietnam Veterans Memorial

One of the most significant efforts to memorialize the Vietnam War is the Vietnam Veterans Memorial in Washington, D.C., designed by architect Maya Lin and completed in 1982. The memorial's stark black granite wall, engraved with the names of the 58,220 American service members who were killed.

Vietnam Veterans Memorial, Washington, D.C.,

Unlike traditional monuments that often celebrate heroism, the Vietnam Veterans Memorial's design is minimal and poignant, emphasizing mourning and remembrance. The memorial was initially controversial due to its unconventional design and perceived lack of patriotic symbolism, but over time it has become one of the most visited and emotionally impactful memorials in the United States.

The memorial plays a vital role in healing for many veterans and their families, providing a place to honor the fallen and recognize the experiences of those who returned. Each year, Veterans Day ceremonies at the memorial draw large crowds, reflecting the ongoing importance of honoring the memory of Vietnam and fostering national reconciliation.

Recognition and Support for Veterans

In the years following the war, Vietnam veterans faced numerous challenges, including a lack of public support and recognition.

In the decades since, however, there has been a significant shift in the recognition and support for Vietnam veterans. Initiatives such as the establishment of the Department of Veterans Affairs (VA) health care centers specifically for Vietnam veterans, as well as increased awareness of PTSD and other mental health issues, have helped provide support for those who served. Public ceremonies and tributes have become more common, and educational programs in schools aim to ensure that future generations understand the sacrifices made by Vietnam veterans.

The National Vietnam War Veterans Day, observed annually on March 29th, is a more recent effort to honor those who served. Established in 2017, the day recognizes the service and sacrifices of Vietnam veterans and addresses the historical lack of appreciation for their contributions.

The Enduring Lessons of Vietnam

The Vietnam War continues to serve as a cautionary tale in American foreign policy and public discourse. Its lessons about the importance of clear objectives, honest communication with the public, and awareness of cultural complexities in foreign countries remain relevant in modern military and diplomatic engagements. The concept of "Vietnam Syndrome," or the reluctance to engage in military interventions without clear purpose or public support, has influenced American foreign policy for decades.

This war also taught Americans the value of a free press and the need for transparency in government. The media coverage of Vietnam exposed the realities of war to the American public in unprecedented ways, which ultimately contributed to the anti-war movement and led to lasting changes in public attitudes toward government and military interventions. The war underscored the need for an informed and engaged citizenry, capable of holding its leaders accountable.

11. REFLECTIONS AND LESSONS OF THE VIETNAM WAR

The Vietnam War stands as one of the most challenging and transformative conflicts in modern American history. Its reverberations have been felt far beyond the jungles of Southeast Asia, affecting American politics, society, and international relations in ways that are still relevant today.

From the intense protests to the haunting experiences of soldiers, from the immense financial costs to the strategic missteps, the war has left a profound legacy that invites reflection and learning.

As we look back, we gain insight into the lessons and consequences of the war and are reminded of the value of understanding history to better shape the future.

I.□*Key Takeaways: Political and Social Lessons*

The Limits of Military Power and Strategic Overreach

One of the big takeaways from the Vietnam War is that military power alone can't always achieve political goals. Even with all its advanced technology and firepower, the U.S. struggled against a determined and resourceful enemy. The war really brought to light how tough it is to fight asymmetric warfare - where a traditional military force faces a guerrilla army that knows the land and has the support of the local population.

Vietnam showed how crucial it is to understand the bigger picture - the politics, culture, and motivations driving the other side. The idea of "winning hearts and minds" was talked about a lot, but it rarely worked in practice. It was a clear reminder that you can't just impose democratic ideals on societies with completely different histories and cultures.

The Role of Media in Shaping Public Perception and Policy

Television brought brutal images of combat and the brutal realities of war directly into American homes. It had a significant role in influencing public opinion. This reporting fueled anti-war sentiment, and raised questions about the war's morality and purpose.

The Vietnam War demonstrated how media coverage could influence political decisions, as public opinion increasingly pressured the government to withdraw. This is still evident today, as media shapes perceptions of conflict, often sparking debate about the responsibilities and limits of journalism in times of war.

The Power and Importance of Public Protest and Civil Activism

The Vietnam War era was marked by one of the most powerful social movements in American history. The anti-war protests not only reflected growing dissent but also showed the impact of grassroots activism on national policy. The protests showed the power of ordinary citizens to influence change, the right of citizens to hold their government accountable and question the decisions that affect their lives and society. The war's unpopularity fueled a wave of activism that set a precedent for future movements.

The Consequences of Ignoring Cultural and Regional Contexts

The war revealed the dangers of overlooking the complexities of foreign cultures and regional politics. Many American policymakers viewed Vietnam through the lens of the Cold War, simplifying the conflict into a binary struggle between communism and democracy. This perspective ignored the nationalist sentiments driving much of North Vietnam's efforts and the local histories and identities that influenced Vietnamese society. Failing to understand the culture, history, and motivations of the Vietnamese people contributed to strategic misjudgements and undermined America's efforts. This lesson continues to resonate, reminding leaders of the importance of a nuanced understanding of the societies they engage with.

The Lasting Impact on Veterans and the Psychological Cost of War

Returning soldiers faced a host of challenges. Their experiences showed just how important it is to address the mental and emotional toll of combat and to help veterans make the transition back to civilian life.

II.▫Quotes from Veterans and Protesters: Reflections from Those Affected

The Vietnam War left profound scars on those who were involved, both soldiers and civilians. Their reflections serve as reminders of the human cost of conflict and the varied perspectives on the war.

- Veteran's Reflection on the Challenges of Combat and Reintegration: "Vietnam was a world of its own - nothing like what we knew back home. Coming back was like entering a different universe. The world had changed, and so had we. But there wasn't much support, just judgment. It took a long time to feel like I was home again." Mike Reynolds, Vietnam Veteran

- Protester's View on Civic Duty and the Anti-War Movement: "We took to the streets not just to end the war, but to be heard, to challenge a system that wasn't listening. The movement wasn't just about peace; it was about justice and the right to question the actions taken in our name." Linda Harper, Anti-War Activist

- Veteran on the Cost of War Beyond the Battlefield: "We lost friends, and we lost parts of ourselves. The things we saw, the things we did - they don't go away. We fought for our country, but sometimes it feels like we came back to a country that didn't want us." Johnathan Davis, Vietnam Veteran

- Protester Reflecting on the Power of Unity: "Seeing people come together - students, parents, veterans - it showed that we weren't alone in questioning this war. The energy of the movement made us believe that we could change things, and in some ways, we did. That unity is something we need to hold onto." Sharon Li, Anti-War Activist

These voices remind us that the Vietnam War was not just a geopolitical conflict but a deeply personal experience for those directly involved. For many, it represented an awakening, a call to action, or a test of endurance, and these reflections highlight the enduring impact of the war on individuals and society.

III. Remembering and Learning from the Vietnam War

As we draw to a close, reflecting on the war is an opportunity to honor those who endured its hardships and to learn from the challenges it posed. The war's legacy reminds us of the cost of conflict, the power of public opinion, and the importance of understanding foreign cultures. It also highlights the responsibility of citizens to question policies that lead to violence and to advocate for peace and justice.

The Vietnam War shaped an entire generation and left a legacy that continues to inform contemporary discussions on military intervention, foreign policy, and the treatment of veterans. By studying this period, engaging with its lessons, and remembering the voices of those who lived through it, we gain a better understanding of the complexities of war and the value of striving for a more peaceful and informed world.

Thank you for reading!

If you enjoyed this book, I would be grateful if you could share your thoughts in a review on Amazon. Thank you!

ABOUT THE AUTHOR

I am a passionate military and history writer whose love for the past was kindled by family stories. One grandfather endured four years as a prisoner of war in Poland during World War 2, while my great-grandfather fought at the Somme in World War 1 — a legacy that ignited a lifelong fascination with courage, conflict, and the human spirit in wartime.

In 2024, after receiving a diagnosis of stage 4 cancer, I turned to writing with newfound purpose. The act of storytelling has become a welcome distraction for me! As of July 2025, I've completed 34 cycles of fortnightly chemotherapy, a treatment that continues — but so does my writing, undeterred and determined.

Whether I'm exploring the battles of World War II, the legends of Greek mythology, the intrigue of Roman emperors, or the ambition of Alexander the Great, I write to inspire curiosity in readers, both young and old, and make history come alive with meaning.

I live in the Cotswolds with my wife, my two children, and two lovely black Labradors. When not writing or reading, you'll likely find me wandering the hills dreaming up my next journey into the past.

See more at: *james-burrows.com and @burrowsauthor*.

If you enjoyed this book, I'd appreciate a review – please scan the QR Code below:

If you'd like to read more, you can find all my books at:

www.ingramcontent.com/pod-product-compliance
Lightning Source LLC
Chambersburg PA
CBHW071212070526
44584CB00019B/3003